To my parents, without whom ...

Batsford Chess Library

How to Play the King's Indian Attack

Angus Dunnington

An Owl Book
Henry Holt and Company
New York

Henry Holt and Company, Inc.
Publishers since 1866
115 West 18th Street
New York, New York 10011

Henry Holt® is a registered trademark
of Henry Holt and Company, Inc.

First published in the United States in 1993 by
Henry Holt and Company, Inc.
Originally published in Great Britain in 1993 by
B. T. Batsford Ltd.

Library of Congress Catalog Card Number: 93-77845

ISBN 0-8050-2933-8 (An Owl Book: pbk.)

First American Edition—1993

Printed in the United Kingdom
All first editions are printed on acid-free paper. ∞

10 9 8 7 6 5 4 3 2 1

Adviser: R. D. Keene, GM, OBE
Technical Editor: Andrew Kinsman

Contents

1 Introduction

Nowadays, it is becoming increasingly difficult at any level of competitive chess to find opponents who know little or – even more rare - no opening theory.

Practitioners of 1 d4 need to be acquainted with defences such as the King's Indian, Grünfeld, Dutch, Benoni, Nimzo-Indian...

Similarly, 1 e4 players will have problems reaching a satisfactory middlegame if they fail to familiarise themselves with, amongst others, the popular Sicilian, French and Caro-Kann Defences. Moreover, each of these is often the opponent's 'pet' line.

Since even masters can take many months (perhaps years) studying the numerous variations of, for example, the Sicilian Defence, it seems logical to find an opening system for White which enables us to sit down at the board before battle commences without having to worry about what Black may play.

This book deals with arguably the most flexible of such systems: the King's Indian Attack (KIA). The beauty of the opening is that White adopts the set-up of ♘f3, g3, ♗g2, d3, ♘bd2 and e4 practically regardless of Black's play (1).

1

When playing the King's Indian Attack the game will follow a course of White's choosing, which should in turn furnish other advantages in the form of extra time on the clock and a 'ready-made' understanding of the positional and tactical nuances which the constraints of a time-limit may prevent the opponent from getting to grips with.

Apart from beginning with 1 ♘f3 or 1 g3 (or even 1 d3), the King's Indian Attack is also a powerful weapon in the hands of 1 e4 players. Therefore fans of 1 e4 openings such as the Ruy Lopez or Scotch need no longer waste their time learning separate lines against Black's other defences, as this system is playable against all of them, the only exception being 1 ... d5, which rules out the King's Indian Attack altogether.

We must also not forget the psychological victory of depriving our opponents the opportunity to show us their encyclopaedic theoretical knowledge of, say, the Caro-Kann when we reply to 1 e4 c6 with 2 d3 and spoil the party immediately (Chapter 4).

Those who play the King's Indian Defence against 1 d4 are strongly advised to take up the same opening when playing White. If it is good with Black, then it must be even better with White! Chapter 7 shows us that the first player can put the extra tempo to good effect.

Before moving on to a deeper discussion of the various aspects of the King's Indian Attack, and Black's most popular ways of meeting it, here are three games which should give the reader an idea of the different paths play might go down in this multi-purpose opening.

White's Kingside Attack

As its name suggests, the King's Indian Attack regularly brings about middlegame positions in which White generates a kingside strike.

A bloodthirsty and illustrative example of this is the following game. Bobby Fischer, the former World Champion, frequently used the King's Indian Attack with success, and here is what can happen if Black plays the French Defence and subsequently takes up White's challenge of a kingside vs queenside attack.

Fischer – U. Geller
Netanya 1968

1	e4	e6
2	d3	d5
3	♘d2 (2)	

Black has a number of ways to try and create play from the diagram position. One is to go for an all-out attack on the queenside in order to counter White's aggression on the other flank, as Black chooses here. This produces very brutal play from both sides, so readers are advised to carefully follow the way in which White conducts his attack, as very similar ideas are used against other Black patterns of development in the French, namely the very popular ... b6 and ... ♗b7, or ... ♗d6 and ... ♘ge7.

It is also possible for Black to exchange in the centre with ... dxe4 at certain stages, although this does not tend to cut across White's plans (See Chapter 3).

3	...	c5
4	g3	♘f6
5	♗g2	♗e7
6	♘gf3	0-0
7	0-0	♘c6
8	♖e1	♕c7
9	e5	♘d7
10	♕e2	(3)

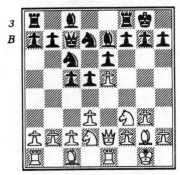

Control of e5 is critical.

10	...	b5
11	h4	

A recurring theme in this particular variation - Black charges forward on the queenside and White endeavours to put as much force as possible into an attack against the opposing king.

11	...	a5
12	♘f1	

Intending ♘f1 - h2 - g4, or in some cases ♘f1 - e3 with sacrificial possibilities on d5 (or f5) - especially when Black has played ... ♕c7.

12	...	♘d4!?

An interesting move, which both prevents a future ♘e3 and opens the c-file for Black's major pieces.

Note that White must capture the knight, as the e-pawn is lost after 13 ♕d1 (not 13 ♕e3 ♘xc2) 13 ... ♘xf3+ 14 ♗xf3 ♘xe5 (15 ♗f4 ♘xf3+).

13	♘xd4	cxd4
14	♗f4	

White's queen's bishop almost always finds itself on f4 in such positions.

14	...	♖a6
15	♘h2!	

Tempting but inaccurate was 15 ♗xd5?! (with the idea of 15 ... exd5 16 e6). After 15 ... ♗b4! White would be forced to play the passive 16 ♖eb1 with equality, since both 16 ♖ec1?? exd5 17 e6 ♖xe6! 18 ♕xe6 ♕xf4! 19 ♕xd7 ♕xc1 and 16 ♖ed1?? exd5 17 e6 ♖xe6 18 ♕xe6 ♕xf4 19 ♕xd7 ♕f3! 20 ♘h2 ♕xd1! win for Black.

15	...	♖c6
16	♖ac1	♗a6?

Threatening to triple on the c-file, but imperative was 16 ... ♕b6, even if it would slow down Black's build-up.

17 &xd5! *(4)*

Fischer sees that this typical 'sacrifice' does indeed work on this occasion.

17 ... exd5

White also stands clearly better after 17 ... &c5 18 &e4! &c8 (not 18 ... &xe5? 19 &xe5 &xe5 20 &xh7+) 19 &f3, hitting the d-pawn.

18 e6 &d8

Now 18 ... &xe6 is pointless as White's queen is defended.

19 exd7 &e6

20 &g4!

Cleverly keeping the initiative. Now 20 ... &xd7 21 &e5! takes advantage of the pin Black put himself in, e.g. 21 ... f6 22 &xd4 or 21 ... &f6 22 &xf6!. Consequently, Black must weaken his kingside in order to take White's advanced d-pawn.

20 ... f5

21 &h5 &xd7

22 &f3

Black's 20 ... f5 has left a gaping hole at e5. His d4-pawn is also weak.

22 ... g6

23 &h6 &f6

24 &xe6 &xe6 *(5)*

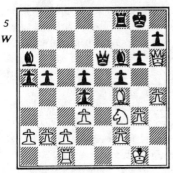

25 &e5!!

There was another way to err here with the natural 25 &e1, as Black could draw by 25 ... &xe1+!! 26 &xe1 &g7! 27 &g5 &f6 etc.

Instead, White eliminates Black's king's bishop, thus gaining total command of the dark squares. Even after 25 moves it is White's control of the important e5-square which decides matters; this over-protection of 'e5' is an essential theme of such positions.

25 ... &xe5

26 &e1 f4

27 &xe5 &d7

Black must avoid 27 ... &g4 28 &e7 &f7 29 &xf7 &xf7 30 &e5+.

28 h5!

Now 28 ... gxh5 loses to 29 &g5+.

28 ... fxg3 *(6)*

29 hxg6!! gxf2+

Against 29 ... &xf3 White has 30 &e8+! &xe8 31 &xh7+ &f8 32 g7+ &e7 33 g8+.

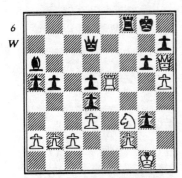

30	&xf2	hxg6
31	₩xg6+	₩g7
32	♖g5!	♖f7

And Black resigned without waiting for either 33 ₩h5 or 33 ₩h6. Incidentally, it is ironic that after 32 ... ₩xg6 33 ♖xg6+ picks up the bishop which was the cause of Black's problems on move 16 (and which never moved again!).

Queenside Expansion

Not surprisingly, White will not always have the pleasure of delivering mate after a crushing kingside attack, as some Black systems encourage the first player to concentrate on seizing an initiative in the centre or on the queenside instead.

In our next game, Croatian Grandmaster Cvitan, a former European Junior Champion, faces the King's Indian Attack and finds himself under pressure on the queenside. He therefore turns to the kingside for counterplay, but we see that White is equally well-placed to defend as well as attack in this particular sector.

**Steinert – Cvitan
Switzerland 1992**

| 1 | ♘f3 | c5 |

Inviting a transposition to a Sicilian Defence. White does eventually oblige, but in his own time and under his own conditions; such is the flexibility of this system.

2	g3	♘c6
3	♗g2	g6
4	0-0	♗g7
5	e4	d6
6	c3	*(7)*

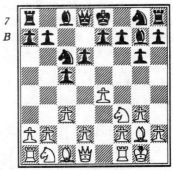

This is a common move in Sicilian positions. Establishing a pawn on d4 would grant White a considerable space advantage, so in order to prevent this Black is provoked into playing his next move:

| 6 | ... | e5 |

Black takes his share of central territory in return for inhibiting his usually influential king's bishop. White is now well placed to profit from the closing of the a1 - h8 diagonal, and he prepares to expand on the queenside with the b2 - b4 push - highlighting another point behind 6 c3.

7	d3	♘ge7
8	a3	

Black has a choice here of either allowing White to carry through his plan or putting a stop to it with 8 ... a5. White meets 8 ... a5 with 9 a4!, after which the lost tempo is a good investment because Black has a hole on b5, which White will use for a knight outpost, usually in conjunction with ♘f3 - d2 - c4.

Since this is not to Black's taste he elects to continue his development instead.

8	...	0-0
9	b4	h6

Preparing ... ♗e6, which White would otherwise counter with ♘g5.

10	♘bd2	♗e6
11	♖b1	b6
12	♗b2	b5!?

If Black continues passively White will simply play to open up the game with ♘d2 - b3 and d3 - d4, perhaps temporarily sacrificing his d-pawn if necessary. Consequently, Cvitan essays to engineer some play to distract his opponent.

13	♖e1	a5
14	a4!	*(8)*

Guaranteeing that a white pawn will reach b5 and subsequently force Black to tread

carefully on the queenside.

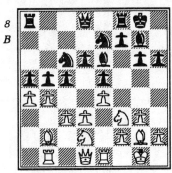

14	...	cxb4
15	axb5	♘a7

15 ... bxc3 16 ♗xc3 followed by ♕a4 not only leaves the black a-pawn susceptible to attack, but also allows White's queen's rook to support his passed b-pawn.

16	c4	g5

Black strives to build up pressure on the other flank.

17	♘f1	

Heading for e3, from where the knight can observe both d5 and f5.

17	...	♘ac8
18	♗c1!	

Note that Black's ostensibly dangerous a- and b-pawns cannot advance. Black first has to defend b4 before he can push with a4, and because of White's strong grip on the light squares on the queenside this is by no means easy to organise.

18	...	♘g6
19	♘e3	♘ce7

Black's only hope is to build up a kingside attack and throw everything at his opponent before White decisively increases his queenside advantage.

20 ♘d2   ♖a7
21 ♖a1 *(9)*

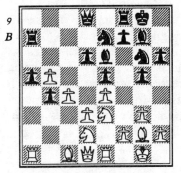

Threatening ♖a4 followed by ♘b3. Black acts quickly.

21 ...   ♘f4
22 ♗f1

Calm play from White as 22 gxf4 exf4 23 ♘c2 ♗xa1 24 ♘xa1 a4 plays into Black's hands.

22 ...   f5
23 exf5   ♘xf5
24 ♘xf5   ♗xf5
25 gxf4

White cannot permit the invading knight to remain in the heart of his position for too long, so he puts the onus on Black to justify the sacrifice.

25 ...   exf4
26 ♖a2   g4
27 ♗b2   ♗xb2
28 ♖xb2   ♕h4
29 ♘e4   ♖g7

Black continues energetically by aiming what is left of his army at the white king, but White's faithful King's Indian

Attack bishop is ready to come to the rescue.

30 ♗g2!   f3
31 ♗f1   a4

Trying to confuse. White ignores the diversionary tactics and consolidates his kingside.

32 ♘g3   b3
33 ♕a1   ♗d7
34 ♕xa4   h5
35 ♕xb3

Now the b-pawn is at last ready to march for promotion.

35 ...   ♕g5

A token threat of ... h5 - h4 before resigning.

36 c5+   ♔h8
37 c6   1-0

The Sicilian Defence is dealt with in Chapter 2.

Positional Themes

Having seen White first mount a formidable kingside attack, then display resilience on this side of the board while simultaneously building up a winning advantage on the queenside, here is a game in which White not only controls both wings but also places his queen on a dominating central square.

This time Black meets the King's Indian Attack with a reliable, positionally-oriented method of development which is perfectly suited to English 'super'-Grandmaster Michael Adams's style (Chapter 5). However, even Adams has problems finding a plan.

**Vaganian – Adams
Ter Apel 1992**

1	♘f3	♘f6
2	g3	d5
3	♗g2	c6
4	0–0	♗g4 *(10)*

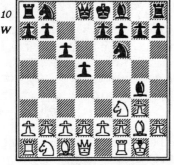

A solid system which immediately solves Black's problem of where to put the queen's bishop, often a problem piece (a similar solution is to play ... ♗f5, which is discussed in Chapter 6). Black can play for ... e5 or settle for ... e6, although in either case the quiet nature of Black's development allows White to obtain a slight but persistent advantage.

5	d3	♘bd7
6	♘bd2	e5
7	e4	dxe4
8	dxe4	♗c5
9	a4	0–0

9 ... a5 is an alternative worth consideration, when the potential weaknesses of Black's a-pawn and the b6-square may prove to be lesser evils than the prospect of permitting White to advance with a4 – a5.

10	h3	♗h5

There is no reason why Black should voluntarily give up the two bishops.

11	a5!?	

The first step in a scheme designed to restrict Black's possibilities on both sides of the board. Tying his opponent down in this way will make it easier for White to embark upon active operations in the middlegame.

11	...	♕c7
12	♕e2	b5

Denying White the use of the effective c4-square.

13	♘b3	♗e7
14	g4	

The time has come to take a kingside initiative, hoping to close the queen's bishop out of the game. The price White pays is the production of a weakness on f4, but he is compensated for this by an outpost himself on f5.

14	...	♗g6
15	♘h4	♘c5
16	♘f5	♘e6

Not 16 ... ♘xb3?! 17 cxb3 when the open c-file provides White with a firing line against Black's c-pawn. Moreover, Black's queen's knight has been given the assignment of keeping watch over f4.

17	♗e3	♖ab8 *(11)*
18	c4	

Now after 18 ... bxc4 19 ♕xc4

the pressure against both a7 and c6 guarantees White a considerable advantage.

Incidentally, exchanging his admittedly passive bishop for the irksome knight is not to be recommended: 18 ... ♘xf5 19 exf5 and White's light-squared bishop comes to life.

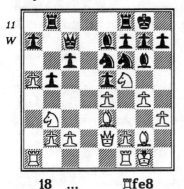

18 ... ♖fe8

Preparing to drop the bishop back to f8.

19 ♖fc1 b4

The unpleasant threat of opening the c-file causes Black to close the queenside. Now Adams has the positional threat of ... c5 followed by ... ♘d4.

20 c5 ♗f8
21 ♕c4

White adds support to d4 and occupies the a2 - g8 diagonal. He also introduces the option of attacking the stranded enemy b-pawn.

21 ... ♖ed8
22 ♖ed1 h5

With no hope of play in any sector of the board, Black attempts to undermine White's hold on the kingside.

23 g5 *(12)*

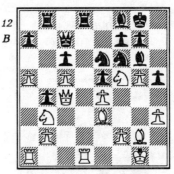

23 ... ♘d5

The obvious alternative is to retreat the attacked knight, but 23 ... ♘h7 24 ♘h4! ♘hxg5 25 ♘xg6 loses material due to 25 ... fxg6 26 ♗xg5. This leads to 23 ... ♘e8 24 ♘h4 (threatening 25 ♘xg6 fxg6 26 ♕xe6+) 24 ... ♕e7 with a miserable position (is 24 ... ♔h7 25 ♘xg6 ♔xg6 possible?). Adams therefore goes for complications. Vaganian's last move took away one of his knight's supporters, which Black hopes to profit from.

24 exd5! cxd5
25 ♖xd5 ♖xd5

Better is 25 ... ♗xf5 with a good game for White thanks to his dangerous queenside superiority.

Now Vaganian has ready a surprisingly strong move which nets him - at this level - a decisive advantage.

26 ♘h4! *(13)*

Underlining the significance of 22 ... h5. After 26 ... ♖dd8 27 ♘xg6 White will have two pieces for a rook, a mighty passed c-pawn and domination of the light squares.

Again Adams tries to throw his opponent off balance.

13
B

26	...	⌷xc5
27	♘xc5	♗xc5
28	♘xg6	♛d6

Or 28 ... ♗xe3 29 ♛xc7 ♘xc7 30 ♘e7+ ♔f8 31 ♘c6!.

29	♗xc5	♘xc5
30	♛d5	♛xd5
31	♗xd5	⌷d8

| 32 | ⌷d1! | 1-0 |

Move order

The observant reader is no doubt aware by now that it is a matter of taste which way White begins the King's Indian Attack – either 1 ♘f3 or 1 e4, depending on what other openings one feels comfortable (or uncomfortable) playing. Whichever the choice, transpositional possibilities abound.

This is particularly evident with the French and Sicilian Defences, and indeed many of the games which begin in one of these may well cross over into the other. Consequently, Sicilian games in which Black plays an early ... d5 are very closely linked to those in the French in which Black advances with ... c5.

2 KIA vs Sicilian Defence

Not unlike the main line of the Sicilian Defence, Black has several continuations, depending on where the d- and e-pawns go. Regardless of the chosen pawn structure Black should post his king's bishop actively by way of a fianchetto. The most economical course is ... d6 and ... ♘f6, waiting for White's reaction before deciding whether or not to claim more territory with ... e5. White is ready to meet the ambitious ... f5 with equally vigorous play, but because of the extra tempo the albeit obvious ♘f3 – e1 and f2 – f4 could give Black problems.

Another idea for White is to expand on the queenside, keeping Black tied down in order to threaten an advantageous breakthrough in the centre. A space advantage on the queenside should also be enough to give White the better prospects in a queenless middlegame if Black seeks a queen trade by opening the d-file with ... d5 and ... dxe4, as in the game Loginov – Madl.

Some players prefer to develop the king's knight on e7 after ... e6, when it can support the queen's knight and give the g7- bishop more freedom to facilitate the ... e5 push.

Black's other main approach is to combine ... e6 and ... ♘ge7 with ... d5. This is similar to the French Defence and appears to be a popular choice. It is difficult to see why, however, because White has a distinct advantage which can easily assume more sizeable proportions. Exchanging on d5 gives White an initiative, while closing the centre with e4 – e5 results in a position in which White has excellent kingside attacking chances.

A note on move order. The fact that the first two games begin with 1 ♘f3 helps show that we can reach a Sicilian without opening 1 e4. Also, after 1 e4 c5 White does not have to play 2 d3, but can instead play 2 ♘f3 and 3 d3. This has the advantage of perhaps committing Black to 2 ... e6 or 2 ... d6. Finally, 1 e4 c5 2 g3 d5 prevents White from adopting a King's Indian Attack set-up.

Fianchetto with ... d6

Smyslov – Botvinnik
USSR Ch 1955

1	♘f3	♘f6
2	g3	g6
3	♗g2	♗g7
4	0-0	0-0
5	d3	c5
6	e4	

Although we have reached a Sicilian Defence, Black could still transpose to a King's Indian Reversed with ... d5 either here or on the next move.

6	...	♘c6
7	♘bd2	d6 (14)

Black develops naturally, for the moment settling for an e7 - d6 - c5 pawn formation. Often ... e5 is played, either voluntarily or otherwise, depending on how badly White wants to build a powerful pawn centre with c2 - c3 and d3 - d4. This idea is considered in more detail in the next game.

8 a4

White gains space on the queenside and prepares ♘c4 (the immediate 8 ♘c4 invites the obvious and effective 8 ... b5!).

8 c3 transposes to Barczay - Forintos, Hungary 1968, when White countered queenside expansion with a central advance: 8 ... ♖b8 9 a4 a6 10 ♕e2 (better than 10 ♖e1 ♘g4!, preventing 11 d4) 10 ... b5 11 axb5 axb5 12 d4 with a slight edge to White.

In the game Larsen - Gligoric, Vinkovci 1971, White dispensed with c2 - c3 altogether and caused Black problems on both sides of the board by marching his wing pawns forward. The game actually went 7 ♖e1 d6 8 ♘bd2, and after 8 ... ♖b8 9 a4 b6 10 ♘c4 ♗b7 11 h4!? was a good try for initiative. There followed 11 ... ♕c7 (11 ... d5 12 exd5 ♘xd5 13 h5!) 12 ♗d2 ♖bd8 13 ♕c1 d5 14 ♗f4! (before trading off the dark-squared bishops Larsen first forces the enemy queen onto a white square) 14 ... ♕c8 15 exd5 ♘xd5 16 ♗h6 ♖fe8 17 ♗xg7 ♔xg7 18 h5! ♘f6 19 h6+ ♔g8 20 ♕f4 ♘h5 21 ♕d2 f6 22 a5! b5 23 a6! with a clear advantage to White.

8 ... ♘e8

An active retreat; Black plans ... f5. Smyslov - Ivkov, Palma Interzonal 1970, saw instead 8 ... ♖b8 9 ♘c4 ♘d7 10 ♘h4! a6 11 f4 b5 12 axb5 axb5 13

♘e3 ♘b6 14 f5 c4 15 ♘g4, when White's attack looked much more dangerous than Black's.

Black chose a dubious plan in Spraggett - Sunye Neto, Manila 1990. After 8 ... b6 9 ♘c4 ♗b7 10 ♖e1 ♖c8 11 c3 he played 11 ... ♘d7 (ruling out 12 d4 because of 12 ... cxd4 13 cxd4 ♘xd4!), but 12 ♘e3 ♘ce5 13 ♘xe5 dxe5? left Black susceptible to a4 - a5 and a later ♘e3 - d5.

9   ♘c4   e5

Gaining more central territory before the ... f5 thrust.

10   c3   f5

One problem with Black's idea is that it is not difficult for White to correctly predict the moves. Consequently Smyslov is ready to meet this rash - if consistent - push. Less ambitious but more accurate is 10 ... h6, preparing 11 ... ♗e6.

11   b4!

A clever pawn sacrifice which takes advantage of the opening of the a2 - g8 diagonal.

Declining with 11 ... f4 is to be considered, when 12 bxc5 dxc5 13 gxf4 exf4 14 ♗a3 ♗xc3 15 ♗xc5 ♗xa1 16 ♗xf8 favours White. The alternative 14 ... b6 seems better, when 15 d4 is unclear.

11   ...   cxb4
12   cxb4   fxe4

Black continues to underestimate White's attacking potential. Once again 12 ... h6 suggests itself. 12 ... ♘xb4, however, is punished by 13 ♕b3!, threatening both the wayward knight and a deadly discovered check.

13   dxe4   ♗e6
14   ♘e3!

Still offering a pawn in order to keep the upper hand.

14   ...   ♘xb4
15   ♖b1 *(15)*

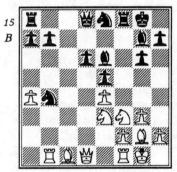

15   ...   a5

15 ... ♘a6 gives White a opportunity to go wrong with 16 ♖xb7?, allowing Black to turn the tables by 16 ... ♘c5 17 ♖b4 a5 18 ♖b1 ♘xe4.

Instead White homes in on the weak light squares in Black's camp, and can even afford to give away his a-pawn, e.g. 15 ... ♘a6 16 ♘d5! ♘c5 17 ♘g5! ♗d7 18 ♗e3 ♗xa4 19 ♕d2 with threats such as 20 ♗xc5 followed by 21 ♘e6, 21 ♖xb7 or 21 ♕a2 (note that 19 ... ♕d7 fails to 20 ♗h3).

16   ♗a3   ♘c7

Black improves the position of his king's knight, as trying to hang onto his extra pawn with 16 ... ♕b6 allows 17 ♘g5.

17	♗xb4	axb4
18	♖xb4	♗h6
19	♖b6!	

White prefers to take the d-pawn. Although Black can defend along the rank by 19 ... ♖a6, White then plays 20 ♖xb7, when the useful manoeuvre ... ♘c7 - a6 - c5 is no longer possible because a6 is already occupied. Black tries to defend energetically.

19	...	♗xe3
20	fxe3	♗c4
21	♖xd6	♕e8
22	♖e1	♖f7

Capturing the a-pawn with the rook runs into difficulties because of (after 22 ... ♖xa4) 23 ♖d7 or 23 ♘xe5. However, 22 ... ♕xa4 looks like an improvement on Botvinnik's choice. After 23 ♕xa4 ♖xa4 24 ♘xe5 White retains his advantage into the ending, but at least Black will not be subjected to the vicious onslaught which follows.

The crucial factor is Black's weakened kingside. The king is without sufficient guard and his pawn cover leaves something to be desired, making him particularly vulnerable on the second rank. Hence his 22nd move.

23	♘g5	♖e7
24	♗f1!	

White has to strike while the iron is hot. Black is now pressured into relinquishing his rule

of the vital a2 - g8 diagonal, since 24 ... ♗a2 25 ♖e2 ♕xa4 26 ♕xa4 ♖xa4 27 ♖xa2 ♖xa2 28 ♘c4+ wins.

24	...	♗xf1
25	♖xf1	

Another benefit of exchanging bishops is the White rook's renewed posting on the f-file.

25	...	♕xa4 *(16)*

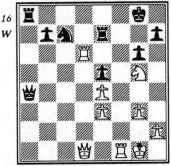

Kicking the knight with 25 ... h6 allows 26 ♖ff6!, when 26 ... hxg5 27 ♖xg6+ is decisive. After 27 ... ♖g7 28 ♖xg7+ ♔xg7 29 ♖d7+ is enough. 27 ... ♔h8 28 ♖h6+ ♔g8 29 ♖dg6+ ♖g7 30 ♕h5 and 27 ... ♔f8 28 ♖df6+ ♖f7 29 ♕d6+ ♕e7 30 ♖xf7+ ♔xf7 31 ♖g7+! are also winning for White.

26	♖d8+!	

Now 26 ... ♖xd8 is not possible because of 27 ♕xa4, whilst 26 ... ♔g7 loses to 27 ♕d6, so Black goes along with White's plan.

26	...	♖e8
27	♕f3!	

Threatening 28 ♕f7+ ♔h8 29 ♕xh7 mate. Black is able to parry this, but his position is beyond repair.

27	...	♛c4
28	♖d7	1-0

There is no way to survive. 28 ... ♖f8 29 ♖xc7! ♛xc7 30 ♛xf8+ ♖xf8 31 ♖xf8+ ♔xf8 32 ♘e6+ and 33 ♘xc7 results in a completely won game for White.

Loginov - Madl
Budapest 1991

1	♘f3	♘f6
2	g3	c5
3	♗g2	g6
4	0-0	♗g7
5	d3	0-0
6	e4	d6
7	c3	♘c6
8	♘bd2	e5

Black gains space and increases her influence in the centre, particularly the d4-square. Having the knight on f6 (instead of e7) does inhibit the push of the f-pawn, but as we saw in the previous game this course of action can sometimes rebound on Black. Another plan is to play ... d6 - d5 at some point, after which White no longer has the option of replying e4 - e5.

9	a3	

Although 8 ... e5 rules out 9 d4 from White, it diminishes the power of Black's dark-squared bishop, so now White can take advantage of this by making use of the fact that 7 c3 also adds support to b4.

9 ♖e1 would transpose to Yudasin - Mascarinas, Manila Interzonal 1990, when after 9 ... ♖e8 White, too, chose queen-side action with 10 a3. There followed 10 ... b5 (intending 11 b4 a5!) 11 a4 b4 12 ♘c4 ♖b8 13 h3 bxc3 14 bxc3 d5 15 exd5 ♘xd5 16 ♛c2 with an edge for White due to his well-placed queen's knight and potential pressure against the two opposing centre pawns. Black went for complications: 16 ... ♘xc3!? 17 ♗b2! (not 17 ♛xc3 e4) 17 ... e4 18 dxe4 ♘d4 19 ♘xd4 cxd4 20 ♗xc3 dxc3 21 ♖ad1, with an unclear position which turned out in White's favour a dozen moves later.

Madl elects to ignore White's queenside aspirations, breaking out in the centre in an attempt to secure equality by exchanging queens.

9	...	d5
10	b4	

Waiting for Black to show her hand. White would be left with weak pawns on c3 and d3 after 10 exd5?! ♘xd5, which also frees Black's position unnecessarily.

10	...	dxe4
11	dxe4	♛d3

Apparently winning a pawn, but White has seen a little further.

12	♗b2 *(17)*	
12	...	♘xe4
13	♘xe4	♛xe4
14	♘d4!	

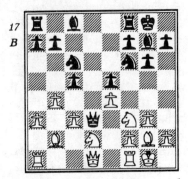

White regains his pawn by unleashing his king's bishop.

    14   ...   ♕g4
    15   ♘xc6   bxc6

Not 15 ... ♕xd1?? 16 ♘e7+.

    16   ♗xc6   ♖b8
    17   ♖e1   ♕xd1
    18   ♖axd1 *(18)*

Black has a couple of vulnerable points on a7 and c5 which leave her struggling for a draw. At the moment White cannot make the capture bxc5 because of the pin on the b-file. However, White should be able to build up enough pressure on the c-pawn to force ... cxb4, when the reply axb4 will allow him to attack the a-pawn along both the a-file and

the g1 – a7 diagonal.

The immediate threat, then, is 19 ♖d5, so Black temporarily prevents this while simultaneously clearing the way for a rook to come to the c-file.

    18   ...   ♗e6
    19   ♘d5   ♗xd5
    20   ♖xd5   ♖fc8

Maintaining the pin on the b-file and thus preserving her c-pawn.

    21   ♖e2   ♖b7

White has rendered the pin useless by defending his bishop, but it is still not possible for him to win a pawn because of 22 ♖xc5 ♖xc5 23 bxc5 ♖c7. Also 22 ♗c1 cxb4 23 axb4 h6! (not 23 ... ♖xc3?? 24 ♖d8+ ♗f8 25 ♗h6) steers White's attention to the defence of his c-pawn and away from ♗e3.

Consequently, White activates his king. Note that Black has problems in utilising her 4-3 kingside pawn majority because White is better placed to react.

    22   ♔f1   ♗f6
    23   ♔e1   ♔g7
    24   ♔d1   h6
    25   ♖e4

White prepares to transfer another rook to attack the enemy c-pawn.

    25   ...   ♖cc7

Anticipating 26 ♖c4, which would now be met by 26 ... cxb4.

    26   ♔c2   cxb4

Since this would have to be

played anyway during the next couple of moves Madl makes the capture at her own convenience.

27 axb4 ♘e7

Black hopes for 28 ♖dxe5 ♘xb4 with instant equality.

28 ♔b3 f6 *(19)*

White has played quite adeptly since the last diagram, making great progress thanks to the king's march to the queenside. His next step towards victory is to exchange off the black defenders and thus simplify the winning process (queening a pawn).

29 ♖c4 ♔f7
30 ♖xc7 ♖xc7
31 ♗c1!

With his king shepherding the queenside pawns it is now possible to redeploy the bishop and attack the black a-pawn.

31 ... ♗e6
32 ♖a5 ♔f5

The a-pawn is lost, and White is about to have two connected passed pawns. Black belatedly hopes for a passed pawn of her own, but her

position is resignable.

33 ♗e3 ♔e4
34 ♖xa7 ♖xa7
35 ♗xa7 f5
36 c4 1-0

White's bishop defends f2 and e3, and he threatens simply to push his c-pawn. Black is much too slow in the race for promotion (note that after 36 ... ♔f3 37 c5 ♔xf2 is even out of the question due to 38 c6+). Remember that Black more or less forced the ending herself by underestimating the power of White's 3-2 pawn majority on the queenside.

The question of move order is interesting here. In the game Yudasin – Mascarinas mentioned in the note to White's ninth move, White played for queenside expansion with a2 - a3 only after the moves ♖e1 and ... ♖e8 had been interpolated (White actually played 7 ♖e1). Loginov's decision to dispense with the perhaps stereotyped rook move has the advantage of tempting the natural but evidently inadequate response of ... d5, ... dxe4 and ... ♕d3.

Psakhis – Erdelyi
Lenk 1991

1	e4	c5
2	♘f3	e6
3	d3	♘c6
4	g3	g6
5	♗g2	♗g7
6	0-0	♘ge7

7	♖e1	d6
8	c3	e5
9	a3	a5

A theoretical novelty. Usually, as we have hitherto seen, Black gets on with his own plans and allows White his queenside initiative. With ... a5 Black gives the game a closed nature, but White can use the self-inflicted weakness on b5 as a home for his queen's knight, even if it costs a tempo.

10	a4	h6
11	♘a3	g5?!

This is quite an ambitious pattern of development, if not a very good one, and readers should be aware of such a possibility when Black has not castled. Preferable is 11 ... 0-0 12 ♘d2! ♗e6 13 ♘dc4 when White stands slightly better.

12	♘b5	♘g6
13	♘d2	

Now if 13 ... 0-0 14 ♘c4 rounds up the black d-pawn, which Black's next is designed to protect.

13	...	♖a6

Played to defend the d-pawn.

14	♘c4	♘ce7
15	b4! *(20)*	

15 d4! also confers White a big advantage. Grandmaster Psakhis opts to keep the central thrust in reserve until he has managed to neutralise the potentially powerful black king's bishop.

15	...	axb4

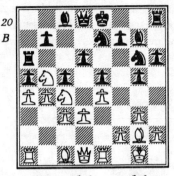

16	cxb4	cxb4
17	♗d2	♗e6
18	♗xb4	

White has succeeded in opening up the queenside, after all. Meanwhile, Black's forces have migrated to the kingside and are sorely missed, and his d-pawn is a weakness which needs defending (18 ... d5 19 ♘cd6+).

18	...	♘c8

18 ... ♗xc4 19 dxc4 opens the d-file in White's favour.

19	♘e3!	

The grandmaster emphasises the folly of Black's opening idea by heading for f5, which would usually be covered by a black g6-pawn.

19	...	0-0

Black manages to tuck his king away before move 20!

20	♘f5	♘ge7

Not 20 ... ♗xf5? 21 exf5 ♘ge7 22 ♗xb7, winning for White.

21	♘xg7	♔xg7
22	d4	

We see that White was correct to wait with this move, as now Black cannot afford to play 22 ... exd4 and open the long diagonal on which his king stands. Consequently, White can keep his pawn on d4 and maintain the tension.

22 ...   ♕b6
23 ♗f1!

Bringing the bishop to a potentially more active post and adding support to the queenside.

23 ...   f6

Black bolsters the dark squares around his king, in particular the a1 - h8 diagonal.

24 ♕d2

White is intent on refraining from committing himself in the centre, even though 24 ♖c1 gives good prospects of increasing his advantage. If Black then chooses to block the c-file with 24 ... ♘c6, White plays 25 d5 ♘xb4 26 dxe6 ♘c6 27 ♘xd6 ♘xd6 28 ♕xd6 ♖d8 29 ♕a3!.

However, White stands much better anyway, and there is nothing wrong in improving his position and pressurising Black a little more.

24 ...   ♘c6
25 a5   ♕d8
26 ♗c3

White prefers to keep his useful queen's bishop on the board rather than allow 26 d5 ♘xb4.

26 ...   ♗g4
27 ♖ec1!

Again Psakhis wants more. 27 d5 ♘6a7 28 ♘a3 wins the

exchange, but Black plays 28 ... f5! with the makings of a dangerous kingside attack, even more potent with White's king's bishop missing.

27 ...   ♕e7
28 ♗b2

A quiet move with a decisive threat of 29 d5 ♘b8 30 ♖c7 ♘d7 31 ♖xb7. Thus Black surrenders his central strongpoint.

28 ...   exd4
29 ♘xd4   ♘e5

29 ... ♘xd4 30 ♗xd4 ♖a8 31 f4 (threatening 32 fxg5 hxg5 33 ♕xg5+) is terrible for Black.

30 ♖a3!

White is commanding the game to such an extent that an effective assault will bring victory. Taking the exchange with ♗xa6 is not necessary at the moment and, in order to remove this possibility, Black must lose valuable time with the retreat which follows.

30 ...   ♖a8
31 f4   ♘f7
32 f5!

Closing Black's bishop out of the game and nailing down the e6-square. White is about to close in.

32 ...   ♘e5
33 ♘e6+   ♔g8
34 ♕d5! *(21)*
34 ...   ♖f7
35 ♖c7   ♕e8
36 ♗xe5   dxe5
37 ♗b5!

This way White forces a win of material for which Black will have no compensation.

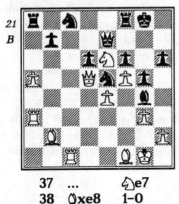

37 ...   ♘e7
38 ♗xe8   1-0

Black plays ... e6 and ... d5

Against the Closed Sicilian Black's most common scheme of development is based on the set-up ... ♘c6, ... g6, ... ♗g7, ... e6 and ... ♘ge7. The system which we now move on to discuss is therefore a common choice with Sicilian players, although it can equally well arise from a French Defence move order.

Dvoretsky – Vulfson
USSR 1986

1	e4	c5
2	♘f3	e6
3	d3	♘c6
4	g3	d5
5	♘bd2	g6
6	♗g2	♗g7
7	0-0	♘ge7 (22)
8	exd5!?	exd5

Black prefers to maintain his pawn centre because the alternative 8 ... ♘xd5 grants White

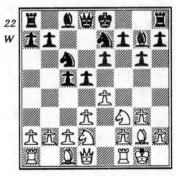

a dangerous initiative. The game Csom – Ivkov, Ljubljana – Portoroz 1973, arrived at a position almost identical to the one above, the only difference being the development of Black's king's knight on f6 instead of e7. Here, too, White played 8 exd5, when Black was obliged to recapture with the knight as 8 ... exd5 9 ♖e1+ is obviously not to be recommended. After 8 ... ♘xd5 the play went as follows: 9 ♘b3 b6 10 c4! ♘de7 11 d4 cxd4 12 ♘fxd4 ♗d7 13 ♗g5 (This would also have been the reply to 12 ... ♗b7. White stands very well – he has a space advantage, more actively posted pieces and an entry square on d6.) 13 ... f6 14 ♗e3 0-0 15 ♕e2 e5 16 ♘b5 ♘f5 17 ♖ad1 ♕e7 18 ♖d2 ♖ac8 19 ♖fd1 and Black was under pressure.

9 d4!?

With his opponent's king still uncastled, White sacrifices a pawn to undermine Black's centre and develop some play on the dark squares. An alternative is 9 ♘b3, delaying the d3 - d4 push until it is fully prepared.

9 ... cxd4

Better than 9 ... ♘xd4?! 10 ♘xd4 ♗xd4 (10 ... cxd4 11 ♘b3 is similar to the game, but the knight exchange leaves Black with fewer chances of counterplay) 11 ♘b3 with a clear plus for White.

10 ♘b3 ♕b6

Black could also hang on to his front d-pawn by playing 10 ... ♗g4, although 11 h3 ♗xf3 12 ♕xf3 gives White good compensation. His next moves will be ♖e1, ♗f4 (or ♗g5) and ♖ad1.

11 ♗g5

Dvoretsky himself gives 11 ♗f4!? - intending ♗d6 - c5 - as a possible improvement. Then 11 ... d3 12 c3 ♗f5 13 ♖e1 0-0 14 ♘h4 ♗e6 15 ♕xd3 is comfortable for White.

Black should continue with his development and meet 11 ♗f4 with 11 ... ♗f5. After the planned 12 ♗d6 0-0 13 ♖e1! ♖fe8 (or 13 ... ♗e4 14 ♗c5 ♕c7 15 ♗xe7 ♘xe7 16 ♘fxd4 ♗xg2 17 ♔xg2, favouring White) 14 ♗c5 ♕c7 15 ♗xd4 White's firm control of the d4-square helps him play against the opposing isolated pawn.

The less incisive game move works out well, but Black has better than his next in 11 ... 0-0 12 ♘fxd4 ♘f5!, effectively neutralising White's edge (e.g. 13 ♘xf5 ♗xf5 14 ♗xd5 ♗xb2).

Note that the string of captures beginning with 12 ... ♘xd4 favours White: 13 ♗xe7 ♘xb3 14 ♗xf8 ♘xa1 15 ♗xg7 ♔xg7 16 ♕xa1.

11 ... ♘f5
12 ♖e1+ ♗e6
13 g4!

White seems prepared to go to any lengths in order to seize control of d4. As for Black, his stranded king is the source of his coming tactical problems.

13 ... ♘d6
14 ♘fxd4!

An imaginative positional sacrifice which tests the Black defences. 14 c3 was tempting, with the idea of 14 ... dxc3 15 ♕xd5!, but 14 ... ♘e4 cuts across White's plan.

14 ... ♗xd4

Or 14 ... ♘xd4 15 ♗e3 ♘6b5 16 a4, tying Black up.

15 ♘xd4 ♕xd4

The best continuation, as 15 ... ♘xd4 16 ♗f6 leaves Black in a dismal position.

16 ♗xd5! *(23)*

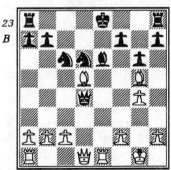

Superb. Black's d-pawns have disappeared and he is

under severe pressure on the two central files (White should avoid 16 ♕xd4? ♘xd4 17 ♗f6 ♘xc2).

16   ...   0-0!

White would also retain his initiative after the exchange of queens, e.g. 16 ... ♕xd1 17 ♖axd1 ♘b5 (if 17 ... ♔d7 18 ♗f4 creates new and equally strong threats on the d-file) 18 ♗f6! (even better than 18 ♗xe6 fxe6 19 ♖xe6+ ♔f7 20 ♖f6+ ♔e8 21 ♖e1+ ♔d7 22 ♖f7+) 18 ... ♖f8 (it was also necessary for White to consider castling: 18 ... 0-0 19 ♖xe6! fxe6 20 ♗xe6+ ♖f7 21 ♖d7, when White will soon reap the benefits of his powerful bind) 19 ♖e3!. White is winning because of the powerful threat of ♗xc6+ followed by ♖ed3 and ♖d8+.

17   ♗xc6   ♕c5!

Again Black continues in the most accurate fashion. Two other tries are clearly inferior: White has much the better endgame after 17 ... ♕xd1 18 ♖axd1 bxc6 19 ♖xd6 ♗xg4 20 ♖xc6; and similarly 17 ... ♕xg4+ 18 ♕xg4 ♗xg4 19 ♗g2 is terrible for Black since his minor pieces are no match for White's raking bishop pair.

18   ♗f3!

An interesting possibility is 18 ♗d5!?, when 18 ... ♗xd5? 19 ♖e5 ♘e4 20 ♗e3 greatly favours the first player. Black is able to obtain good drawing chances, however, with 18 ... ♕xd5! 19

♕xd5 ♗xd5 20 ♖ad1 ♗f3 21 ♖xd6 ♗xg4.

Another 'obvious-looking' move is 18 ♗e7, but Black has a route to equality in 18 ... ♕xc6 19 ♕xd6 ♕xd6 20 ♗xd6 ♖fd8 followed by ... ♗xg4.

White's calm choice is in fact the only way to keep Black on the defensive.

18   ...   ♕xg5
19   ♕xd6   ♖ac8
20   c3   ♕b5!

Black loses a piece after 20 ... ♗xg4? 21 ♕g3 h5 22 h3; while the attempt to win a kingside pawn by first eliminating White's h-pawn is also unsatisfactory: 20 ... h5 21 h3 hxg4 22 hxg4 ♗xg4 23 ♕g3 ♖c4 (on 23 ... f5 White replies 24 ♖e6) 24 ♗xb7 with a comfortable advantage.

20 ... ♖fd8? is weak on account of 21 ♕e5! ♕xe5 22 ♖xe5.

21   ♖ad1   ♗xa2

Not 21 ... ♕xb2? 22 ♖xe6! fxe6 23 ♕xe6+ ♔h8 (or 23 ... ♔g7 24 ♖d7+) 24 ♕e5+ ♔g8 25 ♗d5+.

22   ♖d2   ♖fd8

White was threatening 23 ♖e7, so Black decides to enter into an endgame in which his queen faces two active rooks. On 22 ... ♖fe8 White anyway plays 23 ♖e7! with advantage, e.g. 23 ... ♖xe7 24 ♕xe7 ♖e8 25 ♕xb7 ♖e1+ 26 ♔g2 ♕f1+ 27 ♔g3

If Black brings his bishop back into the game by 22 ... ♗e6 White should harass his opponent's queen with 23 ♖e5! (note that here 23 ♖xe6? fxe6 24 ♕xe6+ ♔h8 does not trouble Black).

23	♕xd8+	♖xd8
24	♖xd8+	♔g7
25	♖d2	

White defends his b-pawn before embarking on a gradual kingside build-up.

25	...	h5!

Correct defence, undermining White's attack. Now the suicidal 26 gxh5?? loses to 26 ... ♕g5+ and 27 ... ♕xd2.

26	h3	♗e6
27	♖e4	a5
28	♖ed4	hxg4
29	hxg4	

White's rooks are more active than Black's queen, so 29 ♗xg4 is possible, when the exchange of the remaining bishops makes the defensive task more difficult for Black.

29	...	♕g5
30	♔g2	b6
31	♖e2	♕c5
32	♔g3	

White improves his position with each move; Black must sit and wait.

32	...	♕b5
33	♖dd2	♕g5
34	♖e3	

This move vacates the e2-square for the bishop and invites the rash advance 34 ... f5? (threatening 35 ... f4+). Although 35 ♖xe6 meets with 35 ... ♕xd2, 35 ♖d4! gives White a distinct pull.

34	...	♕c5
35	♗e2	♕c6?!

Better is 35 ... ♕c7+ 36 ♔g2 ♕c6+.

36	f3?

After nurturing his advantage so well White holds back, letting his opponent off the hook! The planned 36 f4! was called for, with good winning prospects. Perhaps White was afraid of 36 ... ♕h1, but 37 ♖d1! prevents any annoying checks.

36	...	g5!

With this advance Black guarantees a draw since White's potential kingside attack has been nullified. Now White tries a different approach, but his opponent is ready.

37	♖d4	♕c7+
38	♔g2	♔f6
39	♗d3	♕c5
40	♗e4	♕b5
41	♖d2	♕e5
42	♖ee2	♕b5
43	♗b7	♕c5
44	♖d4	b5
45	♖ed2	

With the idea of 46 ♗d5 - White's only remaining winning attempt.

45	...	♔e5!

½–½

An interesting game in which Black defended very well right from the opening. Although White's tactical play was impressive, Dvoretsky's own improvement of 11 ♘f4! certainly makes the central exchange with 8 exd5 a promising idea.

Ciocaltea - Ilijin
Romania 1976

1	e4	c5
2	♘f3	e6
3	d3	d5
4	♘bd2	♘c6
5	g3	g6
6	♗g2	♗g7
7	0-0	♘ge7
8	♖e1	

This normal developing move retains the tension in the centre. White then has the choice of transposing to a standard King's Indian Attack set-up with the e4 - e5 push (as in this case), or preparing a timely exd5.

8	...	0-0
9	e5	*(24)*

Also possible is 9 c3, as played in the game Ljubojevic - Hulak, Rovinj-Zagreb 1975. White obtained a threatening position after the moves 9 ... ♕c7 10 exd5 ♘xd5 (10 ... exd5?! 11 ♘b3 is not good for Black, who will also lose a tempo

after, for example, 11 ... b6 12 ♗f4) 11 ♘c4 b6 12 ♘g5!? ♕b7 13 ♕g4 ♖ad8. Now 14 ♕h3! causes Black considerable problems, e.g. 14 ... h6 15 ♘f3 g5 16 ♗xg5! hxg5 17 ♘xg5.

9	...	♕c7
10	♕e2	b6

Dvoretsky - Ubilava, USSR 1979, saw Black play more energetically by throwing forward his queenside pawns, while White persevered with his kingside build-up: 10 ... a5 11 h4 h6 12 ♘f1 (Consistent, although 12 a4 - slowing Black down on the queenside - comes into consideration) 12 ... a4 13 a3 b5 14 ♘1h2 b4 15 ♗f4 ♔h7 16 ♘g4 ♘g8. With an eye to limiting Black's counterplay before entering into a more critical stage of his attack White played 17 c4!. After 17 ... bxc3 18 bxc3 ♗a6 19 c4! dxc4 20 dxc4 ♖ab8 21 h5! ♔h8 (not 21 ... g5 22 ♗xg5! hxg5 23 ♘xg5+ ♔h8 24 ♕e4) 22 hxg6 fxg6 23 ♘f6! White had found his way into his opponent's camp and was well on the way to victory.

11	♘f1	♗a6
12	♗f4	

12 h4 transposes to Dvoretsky - Khalifman, USSR 1987. Black eschewed completing his development and instead tried the unusual 12 ... ♘d4!? 13 ♘xd4 cxd4 14 ♗f4 ♘c6 (If 14 ... ♖ac8 15 ♖ac1 is better for White) 15 a3 ♕d7 16 ♘h2 ♖ae8, intending to challenge White's

e-pawn with ... f6. White happily waited for this imprudent
break: 17 ♘g4 f6 (or 17 ... h5 18
♘f6+ ♗xf6 19 exf6 ♚h7 20 ♘e5!,
keeping White firmly in control
of the all-important e5-square)
18 exf6 ♗xf6 19 ♘xf6+ ♖xf6 20
♘h3! with a terrible game for
Black.

| 12 | ... | ♖ad8 |
| 13 | h4 | d4 *(25)* |

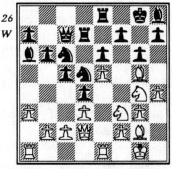

Black would like to use d5
for one of his knights. Another
idea of ... d5 - d4 is to be able
to play ... c5 - c4 without White
closing the centre by d3 - d4.

| 14 | ♘1h2 | ♘b4 |
| 15 | ♕d2! | |

A good dual-purpose move
which prevents the planned 15
... c4 and also adds power to
White's grip on the dark
squares around the enemy king.

| 15 | ... | ♖fe8 |

On 15 ... ♘bd5 White replies
16 ♗h6 and Black must trade in
his only defender of f6 and h6.
Such an exchange would be
disastrous for Black, especially
since White's queen and knights
are ready to pounce.

16	♘g4	♘ed5
17	♗h6!	♗h8
18	♗g5!	♖d7
19	a3	♘c6 *(26)*

A brief study of the diagram
position reveals that, although
Black's pieces seem to be reas-
onably well posted, his failure
to work up any notable queenside pressure has given White
carte blanche on the kingside.

It is also important that the
reader appreciates how White
profited from inserting the
move 17 ♗h6! (forcing 17 ...
♗h8), rather than immediately
playing the automatic 17 ♗g5.
Black's bishop may be 'safe' on
h8, but it no longer has any
influence on the h6-square
(unlike White's). Also, the black
king is now without the useful
flight square in the corner.
These factors combine to give
White a decisive advantage.

Quite often in those systems
in which Black opts for the
fianchetto of his king's bishop
it appears that White is able to
invade quite effortlessly. This
game is no exception, with

White playing standard King's Indian Attack moves, and subsequently finding himself in an overwhelming position.

20 ♘f6!

Threatening to win a piece with 21 ♘h6+. Black's next is forced, as 20 ... ♗xf6 21 exf6 ♔h8 22 ♕h6 ♖g8 23 ♘g5 is final. Nor does 20 ... h5 put up any resistance: 21 ♕h6 ♘xf6 22 ♘xf6+ ♗xf6 23 exf6 followed by 24 ♕g7 mate.

20 ... ♘xf6
21 exf6 h5

On 21 ... ♕d8 comes 22 ♕h6! ♗xf6 23 ♘g5!, unleashing the white bishop.

22 ♘h6+! ♔f8

Not 22 ... ♔h7 23 ♘g5+ ♔xh6 24 ♘xf7+ (better than 24 ♘xe6+ – the king always makes better prey than the queen!) 24 ... ♔h7 25 ♕h6+ ♔g8 26 ♕xh8+ ♔xf7 27 ♕g7 mate.

23 ♘g5

With the audacious threat of 24 ♘h7 mate.

23 ... ♗xf6

If 23 ... ♖c8 (intending 24 ♘h7+ ♔e8) White has 24 ♘hxf7! (threatening to win the queen with 25 ♘xe6+), or 24 ♖xe6!.

24 ♘h7+ ♔g7
25 ♘xf6 ♔xf6 *(27)*

Black has defended quite cleverly to reach the above position. He hopes to simply drop the brave king back to g7 and force White to defend the stranded knight with g3 – g4 –

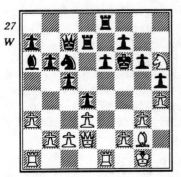

g5, when Black will then use his extra pawn.

However, White's play has been very logical so far, and he has, in fact, seen further than his opponent. The black king is bereft of defence on the dark squares and currently stands outside the fortress, so White should have something ...

26 ♘f5!!

A wonderful move which nevertheless is the culmination of White's skilful play. Unfortunately for Black, the only way to avoid 27 ♕g5 mate leaves White the exchange up (26 ... gxf5 and 26 ... ♔xf5 both meet with 27 ♕g5 mate). If Black ignores the proffered knight with 26 ... e5 he meets with a humiliating end after 27 ♕g5+ ♔e6 28 ♘g7+ ♔d6 29 ♕f6+ ♖e6 30 ♘e8 mate!

26 ... exf5
27 ♖xe8 ♔g7
28 ♖ae1 ♘d8

Apart from being ahead on material, White also has a menacing initiative. Black's king, too, is still not completely safe. Black's last move hopes to hamper the harmony of White's rooks with ... ♘e6.

29 ♕g5! c4

If 29 ... f6 30 ♖g8+! ♔xg8 31 ♕xg6+ ♖g7 32 ♖e8 mate, whilst the intended 29 ... ♘e6 loses to 30 ♖1xe6! fxe6 31 ♖xe6, when Black cannot defend against 32 ♕xg6+.

30 ♖h8!

Yet another 'sacrifice' with which to trouble Black's king. Now 30 ... ♔xh8 31 ♕h6+ ♔g8 32 ♖e8+ is mate, so Black struggles to survive with:

30 ... ♘e6
31 ♕h6+ ♔f6

Once again the black king has been forced to run to f6, but this time there is no escape.

32 ♖e8! 1-0

There is no defence to 33 ♕h8+ ♘g7 34 ♖g8. Black loses a rook after 32 ... ♖d8 33 ♕h8+ ♘g7 34 ♖xd8 (still threatening ♖g8), retreating with 32 ... ♘g7 allows 33 ♕g5 mate.

A fine example of how White can infiltrate the weaknesses around Black's king, particularly when Black fianchettoes his king's bishop.

When Black refrains from early castling White does best to avoid committing himself by e4 - e5, and instead temporise with useful moves such as h4 and c3. The next game is a good example of this strategy in action.

Yudasin – Jukic
Bern 1989

1	e4	c5
2	♘f3	e6
3	d3	♘c6
4	g3	d5
5	♘bd2	g6
6	♗g2	♗g7
7	0-0	♘ge7
8	♖e1	b6

More flexible than 8 ... 0-0. Since the move ... b6 occurs quite frequently in this variation, it seems correct to play it immediately and await White's intentions.

Interesting is 8 ... h6, hoping for the dubious 9 e5? g5! followed by ... ♘g6, surrounding White's e-pawn.

9 h4

9 c3 ♗a6 10 ♘f1 was tried in Minic - Marjanovic, Bor 1980, but 10 ♕a4! transposes to the note to Black's 10th move, without the moves h2 - h4 and ... h7 - h6. Dolmatov - A. Sokolov, Manila Interzonal 1990, saw a trade of queens advantageous to White after 9 c3 a5 10 ♘f1!? dxe4 11 dxe4 ♕xd1.

Another, less popular alternative is 9 a3!?, but this hardly troubles Black.

9 ... h6

Otherwise White may push further with h4 - h5, which Black no longer has to worry about because of the reply ... g6 - g5.

10 c3 a5!

A good move, gaining space

on the queenside (also threatening ... a5 - a4), and preparing to flee from the dangerous h1 - a8 diagonal. The latter wish could be fulfilled by ... ♖b8, but ... ♖a7 is potentially more active.

If Black essays the active 10 ... ♗a6, then 11 ♕a4!? is a trappy alternative to 11 ♗f1. The capture 11 ... ♗xd3 runs into 12 exd5, when 12 ... exd5 and 12 ... ♕xd5 lose to 13 ♕xc6+ and 13 ♘e5 respectively (on 12 ... b5 13 ♕a6 maintains the winning position). Black's best, therefore, is 11 ... ♗b7 or 11 ... ♕c8, hoping that White's queen will be misplaced on a4.

11   a4 *(28)*

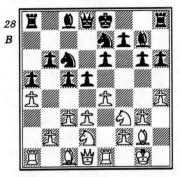

White claims some space of his own and also fixes Black's queenside pawns.

11   ...   ♖a7

In Benjamin - Eingorn, St. John Open 1988, Black played 11 ... ♗a6. After 12 exd5! he kept White's queen's knight out of c4 with 12 ... exd5, but White had no problem in finding another course: 13 ♘b3 0-0 14 d4 c4 (14 ... cxd4 15 ♘bxd4 is

strategically losing for Black due to the isolated d-pawn and the weak-points at b5 and b6) 15 ♘bd2 and White stood much better. Black had to bring his bishop back into the game with ... ♗c8 - e6, while White simply opened up the queenside with a timely b3 followed by putting pressure on Black's b-pawn.

12   exd5!

An improvement over Ljubojevic - Kasparov, Niksic 1983, where White allowed his opponent to effectively close the centre after 12 ♘b3?! d4! 13 cxd4 cxd4 14 ♗d2? (imperative was 14 e5) 14 ... e5! when Black already had a slight edge.

Indeed Black quickly converted his space advantage into a win: 15 ♘c1 (Another try is 15 h5) 15 ... ♗e6 16 ♖e2 0-0 17 ♗e1 f5 18 ♘d2 f4! 19 f3 fxg3 20 ♗xg3 g5! 21 hxg5 ♘g6! 22 gxh6 ♗xh6 23 ♘f1 ♖g7 24 ♖f2 ♗e3! (winning, as 25 ♘xe3 dxe3 26 ♖f1 ♕g5 27 ♘e2 ♘f4 is crushing) 25 b3 ♘f4! 0-1.

This game should be an important lesson – White must play either the space-gaining e4 - e5 or generate pressure on the e-file by exd5. Thus 12 e5 is possible, with a view to concentrating on a kingside build-up. Black can expand on the queenside by 12 ... ♗a6 13 ♘f1 b5, but White's sound pawn structure and possibility of a kingside attack give him an excellent game.

| 12 | ... | **exd5** |

12 ... ♘xd5 13 ♘c4 grants White a useful outpost.

| **13** | **♘b3!** | **d4** |

Black does not want to be left with a fixed backward or isolated pawn on d5 after d3 – d4 from White, so he pushes forward himself. However, White is well placed to encroach upon the weaknesses in Black's camp. Note the power of the g2-bishop.

14	**cxd4**	**cxd4**
15	**♗f4**	**0-0**
16	**♘e5!**	

White is quite happy to make a couple of exchanges as he will then possess a group of harmoniously developed, active pieces compared with Black's scattered forces.

16	...	**♘xe5**
17	**♗xe5**	**♗xe5**
18	**♖xe5**	**♕d6**
19	**♕e2**	**♗e6**
20	**♘d2**	

White regroups his knight, observing the squares c4 and e4.

| **20** | ... | **♘c6** *(29)* |

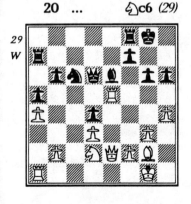

| **21** | **♖xe6!** | |

White's command of the game and the disarray of the opposing pieces combine to make this positional exchange sacrifice worthwhile. Now 21 ... ♕xe6? 22 ♕xe6 fxe6 23 ♗xc6 wins for White, so Black's next is forced.

| **21** | ... | **fxe6** |
| **22** | **♘c4** | **♕d7** |

Black must defend both c6 and e6 (e.g. 22 ... ♕c5 23 ♕xe6+).

| **23** | **♘xb6** | **♕e8** |

Not a desirable move for a queen, although at least Black covers c6, e6, and g6 simultaneously. 23 ... ♕c7 tempts White into 24 ♕xe6+ ♔g7 (24 ... ♔h7 25 ♖c1! ♕xb6 26 ♖xc6) 25 ♕xc6 ♕xc6 26 ♗xc6, when 26 ... ♖f6 is fine for Black. Instead White has 25 ♘d5!, e.g. 25 ... ♕d7 26 ♘f4 with a decisive advantage (26 ... ♘e7 27 ♕xd7 ♖xd7 28 ♘e6+; or 26 ... ♖xf4 27 ♕xd7+ ♖xd7 28 ♗xc6). The other try, 23 ... ♕d6, allows the white knight to return to c4 with tempo.

| **24** | **♖c1** | **♘e7** |

On 24 ... ♖c7 25 ♕e4 wins. Less drastic than the game move is the retreat 24 ... ♘d8, but this reduces Black to passivity in a position in which White has already collected one pawn for his exchange. White could answer 25 ♕e5 and 26 ♕xd4, leaving Black in a hopeless state, with four weak pawns still to defend.

25	♕xe6+	♕f7
26	♕e2	♕b3

Black strives for counter-play, but White now capitalises on the black queen's sortie, also taking advantage of Black's 'hanging' rook and knight.

27	♘c4	♕xa4
28	♕e6+	♔g7
29	♕b6!	♖d7
30	♘e5	♖dd8

On 30 ... ♖f6 31 ♕c5 Black finds his queen's rook with no squares on the second rank – thanks in no small part to White's all-powerful King's Indian Attack bishop.

31	♖c7	♕e8

The queen unceremoniously returns to e8 as White threatened 32 ♕xg6+ as well as 32 ♖xe7+.

32	♕e6	1-0

White's troublesome initiative persisted from 14 cxd4 right through to the end of the game. The open lines and exchanging of key defensive pieces accentuated Black's problems in protecting the numerous defects in his position.

3 KIA vs French Defence

1	e4	e6
2	d3	d5
3	♘d2 (30)	

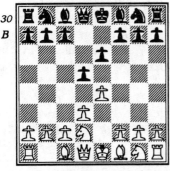

4	♘gf3	♘c6
5	g3	♘f6
6	♗g2	♗e7
7	0-0	0-0
8	♖e1 (31)	

1 e4 players are bound to meet the French Defence quite often, and 2 d3 is an excellent way of steering the game into lesser-known channels.

The 'Long' Variation

The standard variation is one in which Black decides to weather the storm and allow White an all-out kingside attack in return for counterplay on the other flank, and is characterised by the following sequence of moves:

1	e4	e6
2	d3	d5
3	♘d2	c5

This line offers play for both sides and an understanding of the respective attacking and defending themes is crucial, as they are relevant in more than just this variation. As a prelude to the coming kingside onslaught, White will close the centre by pushing with e4 - e5, subsequently chasing away Black's f6-knight and, in fact, leaving Black with a distinct lack of minor piece protection for his king.

Since the advanced e-pawn is such an important part of White's plans, it is imperative that White over-protect it in order to minimise the chance of Black essaying the undermining ... f6. The queen's knight can, after h2 - h4, make the man-oeuvres ♘d2 - f1 - h2 - g4 or ♘d2 - f1 - e3. The latter is especially threatening when Black has played ... ♕c7 and White the usual ♗f4, as this introduces the possibility of playing ♘xd5 followed by e5 - e6. Leaving the h-pawn on the fourth rank helps support the g5-square for when White plays ♘g5 or ♗g5, but pushing further with h4 - h5 has the advantage of inducing Black to either produce a target by ... h6 or allow the creation of a hole on f6 after h5 - h6 from White.

As for Black, the idea is simply to roll the queenside pawns down the board and force White to make positional concessions which hasten Black's queenside attack. Marching the a-pawn all the way to a3 in conjunction with ... b5 - b4 is one good plan, whence White will lose con-siderable control over c3 and d4 - opening the way for the black knights. Another, more access-ible, knight outpost is d5, which Black will make available by playing ... d4.

Not surprisingly, this line produces exciting games, with both players endeavouring to deliver the first knockout blow. Defending the king, however, is

not to everyone's taste, and a slight error from Black may have more serious consequen-ces than one from White. It is for this reason that White has more fun.

Fischer - Miagmasuren
Sousse Interzonal 1967

(from diagram 31)

| | 8 | ... | b5 |

Black wastes no time in setting his queenside pawn roller into action; the slower 8 ... ♕c7 was discussed in the introductory chapter to this book.

9	e5	♘d7
10	♘f1	a5
11	h4	b4
12	♗f4	a4

Developing the queen's bishop with 12 ... ♗a6 adds force to the queenside and makes up for being less chal-lenging by being more flexible. White has two main ways to continue: 13 h5 (13 ... h6 14 ♘e3 followed by ♘g4 and ♕d2 with a view to sacrificing on h6); or 13 ♘g5 and 14 ♕g4.

| 13 | a3! |

Fischer is happy to 'waste' a move on this side of the board because now Black no longer has the useful ... a3 push at his disposal.

13	...	bxa3
14	bxa3	♗a6
15	♘e3	♘a5

Gheorghiu - Uhlmann, Sofia

1967, went instead 15 ... ♘d4 16 c4! ♘b3. Rather than move his attacked rook, White trusted in his attacking opportunities and put his opponent under immediate pressure with 17 cxd5!?. After 17 ... ♘xa1 18 ♕xa1 exd5 19 ♘xd5 ♗xd3? (19 ... ♘b6 is a big improvement) White played 20 e6!. The game ended 20 ... ♘f6 (20 ... fxe6 21 ♗c7 ♕f6 22 ♕c1 ♕c8 23 ♖xe6 threatens ♖xf6! and ♘e7+) 21 ♘xe7+ ♕xe7 22 ♘e5 ♗g6 23 ♘c6 ♕b7 24 ♗d6 ♗e4 25 ♖xe4! ♕xc6 26 ♗xf8 1-0 (26 ... ♖xf8 27 ♕xf6! gxf6 28 ♖g4+; or 27 ... ♕xe4 28 ♕xf7+).

Miagmasuren's ... ♘a5 takes the knight away from the centre (and further from the kingside), and Black will come to regret taking such a luxury.

16 ♗h3!

Dissuading Black from challenging the e5-pawn by ... f6.

16 ... d4
17 ♘f1! (32)

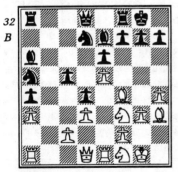

White shows his understanding of these positions with this retreat. Many players would use the g4-square for

the knight, but then White's queen would have difficulty when the time comes to swing over to the kingside.

17 ... ♘b6
18 ♘g5 ♘d5
19 ♗d2

Fischer does not want to exchange his queen's bishop because his g5-knight is menacing enough to push Black into giving up his own dark-squared bishop. Keeping watch over the squares f6 and h6 is vital. Now 19 ... h6 meets with 20 ♘xe6 fxe6 21 ♗xe6+ ♔h8 22 ♗xa5 ♕xa5 23 ♗xd5, highlighting a drawback of 15 ... ♘a5.

19 ... ♗xg5
20 ♗xg5 ♕d7
21 ♕h5 ♖fc8
22 ♘d2 ♘c3
23 ♗f6! (33)

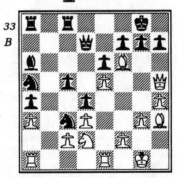

White launches the final attack, against which there seems to be no adequate defence. All of Black's pieces - except his king! - stand helplessly by on the queenside.

23 ... ♕e8

Acceptance of the 'sacrifice'

brings no joy: 23 ... gxf6 24 exf6 ♗h8 25 ♘f3 ♘d5 (25 ... ♖g8 26 ♘e5! threatens both ♘xd7 and ♘xf7+) 26 ♘g5! ♘xf6 27 ♕h6 ♕e7 28 ♗f5! ♖g8 29 ♘xh7.

24 ♘e4!   g6

Black will have to play this move eventually.

25 ♕g5   ♘xe4
26 ♖xe4   c4
27 h5!

White must strike while the iron is hot.

27 ...   cxd3
28 ♖h4!   ♖a7

Hoping to defend along the second rank. Certainly not 28 ... dxc2 29 hxg6 c1=♕+ 30 ♖xc1 ♖xc1+ 31 ♔h2! fxg6 32 ♖xh7! ♔xh7 33 ♕h4+ ♔g8 34 ♕h8+ ♔f7 35 ♕g7 mate.

29 ♗g2!

Now White can meet 29 ... ♕f8 with 30 ♗e4! followed by breaking through the enemy's kingside with hxg6 and ♗xg6, whilst the challenge 29 ... ♗b7 cuts off the a7-rook, allowing 30 hxg6 fxg6 31 ♖xh7.

29 ...   dxc2
30 ♕h6   ♕f8 *(34)*

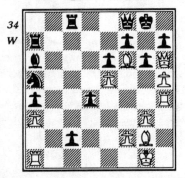

31 ♕xh7+! 1-0

31 ... ♔xh7 32 hxg6+ ♔xg6 33 ♗e4 mate.

Black plays ... b6

As we have seen, White's forces are perfectly posted to carry out a lethal kingside attack, so some black players may prefer to dispense with the advance of the queenside pawns and settle for the more circumspect ... b6 and ... ♗b7.

When Black delays kingside castling the ... b6 strategy deters White from pushing e4 – e5 prematurely, as the e-pawn may become a weakness and Black could take advantage of the closed centre by castling queenside and aiming for the ... g5 thrust to undermine White's kingside defences and reduce White's protection of the e5-pawn. So White often reacts by temporising, waiting for Black to make a commitment before acting in the centre.

A disadvantage of playing waiting moves in order to avoid coming under an early attack is that the opponent is given too much time, and can simply strengthen his position. Here White manages to support his centre with c3 and d4.

**Psakhis – D. Paunovic
Minsk 1986**

1   e4   c5

2	♘f3	e6
3	d3	♘c6
4	g3	d5
5	♘bd2	♘f6
6	♗g2	b6
7	0-0	♗b7
8	♖e1	♗e7 *(35)*

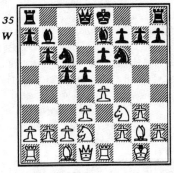

9 a3!?

With this useful move White waits to see where the black king will go. He also retains the possibility of a favourable central exchange with exd5.

9 ♕e2 may transpose to normal lines with e4 – e5, unless Black plays the critical 9 ... ♘b4. After 10 e5 ♘xc2 11 exf6 ♗xf6, Mark Tseitlin – Polovodin, USSR 1981, went 12 ♖b1 ♘xe1 13 ♕xe1 ♗a6 14 ♘e5 0-0 15 ♗f1 ♕c7 16 ♘g4 ♗e7 17 ♘f3 ♖ae8 when the position was unclear.

In the game Kochiev – Legky, USSR 1984, White dispensed with 12 ♖b1 in favour of 12 ♘f1!?. Black played 12 ... ♘xa1 (if 12 ... ♘xe1 13 ♕xe1 ♗a6 14 ♕e2 0-0 15 ♘e3 is slightly better for White) 13 ♗f4 c4 14 d4! ♘b3 15 axb3 cxb3 16 ♕b5+ ♕d7 17 ♕xb3 0-0 18 ♘e3 and

White stood a little better because of his active knights.

9	...	♕c7
10	c3	0-0

10 ... 0-0-0 11 e5 ♘d7 12 d4 as in Hort – Lobron, Bad Kissingen 1981, allows 12 ... g5 with a double-edged game. Instead, White should settle for a slight advantage after 11 ♕e2. Black does well to avoid 10 ... a5?! 11 a4! which favoured White in Knezevic – Jovcic, Yugoslavia 1975.

11	e5	♘d7
12	d4 *(36)*	

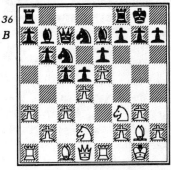

Having played 10 c3, White can now support e5 with a pawn rather than the more usual ♕e2, ♘f1 and ♗f4. The a3-pawn defends the b4-square, ready for the following exchange.

12	...	cxd4
13	cxd4	♘a5

In anticipation of a White kingside attack, Black seeks active play down the c-file. With this in mind, White could now play 14 ♘b1!? followed by 15 ♘c3, but instead Psakhis prefers to concentrate on kingside operations, judging that Black's play on the queen-side will not be too troubling.

14 ♘f1   ♖fc8
15 b4!

White must prevent ... ♛c2. The attempt to do this with 15 ♘e3 is not promising as after 15 ... ♘c4 16 ♘g4 h5!? 17 ♘e3 ♘xe3 18 ♗xe3 ♛c2 Black still achieves his goal.

After the game move Black will have an unchallenged knight on c4 which, unfortun-ately, may serve to only hamper his major pieces and, conse-quently, not distract White from building up pressure on the other flank.

15 ...   ♘c4
16 h4   b5

A necessary move if Black wants to open the queenside. The immediate 16 ... a5 meets with 17 b5!.

17 ♘g5

Wasting no time in begin-ning the attack.

17 ...   a5?!

Black must look for coun-terplay, but chasing the danger-ously hovering knight with 17 ... h6 would at least prevent White from hurling his queen into the heart of battle.

However, in answer to 17 ... h6 White's attacking chances by no means diminish after 18 ♘h3 followed by ♛g4 and ♘f4. Even 18 ♘xf7!? ♔xf7 19 ♛h5+ may be worth a try, as the

remaining cover around the black king could eventually be wiped away with the sacrifice ♗xh6.

18 ♛h5!   ♗xg5

White threatened both 19 ♛xf7+ and 19 ♛xh7+, so Black has no choice but to give up the 'minor exchange' of the two bishops. This has serious con-sequences - the black-squared bishop will be sorely missed once White has pin-pointed the weaknesses in Black's kingside.

19 ♗xg5   axb4
20 axb4   ♖a4
21 ♘h2! (37)

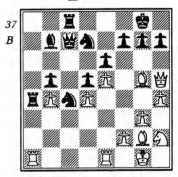

A move which emphasises the simplicity of the King's Indian Attack. After guarantee-ing that the queenside is suffi-ciently safe White makes logi-cal, simple threats on the kingside, inducing important positional concessions which may later be taken advantage of. In the present game White finds that his forces are so well placed that he is able to 'ignore' minor threats on the queenside - often the best that

Black can come up with – and make more powerful threats of his own on the kingside.

If Black now carries out the threatened 21 ... ♖xb4 White plays 22 ♘g4 with the idea of ♗e7 and ♘f6+. The king's bishop will also play a part in the attack with ♗g2 - f1 - d3. Consequently, Black sees time as a more important factor than material and, after strengthening his command of the a-file, brings his knight over to help defend.

21	...	♖ca8
22	♖ab1	♘f8
23	♕g4!	

Making way for the h-pawn, in order to follow with h5 and ♗f6. Should Black now escape the pressure on the g-file with 23 ... ♔h8, White obtains a winning attack: 24 h5 h6 25 ♗f6! gxf6 26 exf6.

23	...	♕c8
24	h5	♘d7
25	h6!	

White thematically forces a further weakening of the dark squares around his opponent's king.

25	...	g6
26	♕h4	

Threatening simply 27 ♘g4, ♗e7 (depriving Black's king of the f8-square) and ♘g4 - f6.

26	...	♕e8
27	♗e7	♗c8
28	♘g4	f5

White threatened 29 ♘f6+ ♘xf6 30 ♕xf6 mating. Another

way of preventing this – less drastic than the game – is 28 ... ♔h8, but Black's days are still numbered.

29	exf6	♕f7
30	f4	

Black also has problems after 30 ♘h2, heading for g5 via f3.

30	...	♘b8

The best defensive try, intending ... ♘c6. White's reaction is violent, giving his opponent no respite.

31	f5!	gxf5

Or 31 ... exf5 32 ♘h2! followed by ♘f3-g5.

32	♗xd5!	(38)

A position worthy of a diagram!

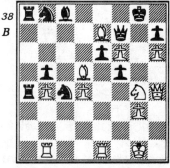

38
B

Black has five pieces on the queenside which are playing no part in the game whatsoever. Only the queen has come to the aid of the king. As for White, his pieces could hardly be better posted. Two pawns have even found their way into Black's kingside.

It is not accidental that White is excellently and Black

terribly placed. Moreover, the diagram position has arisen from active, positionally-oriented play from White who, unlike his opponent, has used the development of his pieces to maximum effect.

32 ...   exd5

Accepting the other piece with 32 ... fxg4 does not help. White brings an end to the game swiftly by 33 ♖xe6! ♗xe6 34 ♕g5+ ♔h8 (or 34 ... ♕g6 35 ♗xe6+ ♔h8 36 f7) 35 ♕g7+! ♕xg7 36 fxg7+ ♔g8 37 ♗xe6 mate.

33 ♕g5+   ♕g6
34 ♕xg6+   hxg6
35 f7+

White jettisons his two far-advanced pawns to continue the mating attack.

35 ...   ♔xf7
36 h7   ♔g7
37 ♗f6+   ♔xh7
38 ♖e7+   ♔g8
39 ♘h6+   ♔f8
40 ♖f7+   1-0

Black resigned, in view of 40 ... ♔e8 41 ♖e1+ mating. The King's Indian Attack is aptly named!.

As will be seen later in this chapter, attacking White on the kingside with the ... g5 thrust can be effective against unprepared opponents. Usually, however, White has already played e4 - e5. In the next game American Grandmaster Yasser Seirawan wrongly predicts this advance and plays ...

h6, but Hodgson has other ideas.

Hodgson - Seirawan
Wijk aan Zee 1986

1	e4	e6
2	d3	d5
3	♘d2	♘f6
4	♘gf3	c5
5	g3	b6
6	♗g2	♗b7
7	0-0	♘c6
8	♖e1	♗e7
9	c3	(39)

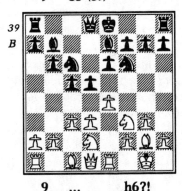

9 ...   h6?!

Not as useful as 9 ... ♕c7. White has not yet committed himself with e4 - e5, so the prospect of the thrust ... g7 - g5 is still quite remote. Consequently, Black has simply weakened his kingside.

In the game Geller - Bagirov, USSR Ch 1963, Black considered waiting moves unnecessary and played 9 ... 0-0. Castling so early is unwise, and after 10 e5 ♘d7 11 ♘f1 ♖e8 12 h4 White was well in command. There followed 12 ... f6 13 exf6 ♗xf6 14 d4! ♖c8 15 ♗g5 cxd4 16 cxd4 ♘a5 17 b3 ♗a6 18 ♘e3! with a nice position for White, whose control of e5 after ♘g4 will secure a lasting advantage.

In the diagram position Black may give the game a different character than the usual closed centre and flank attacks by relieving the tension with 9 ... dxe4. This happened in Petursson - Fehr, Bern 1991, which continued 10 dxe4 e5 11 ♘c4 ♕c7 (11 ... ♕xd1 12 ♖xd1 ♘xe4 13 ♖e1! is bad for Black) 12 ♘e3 ♖d8 13 ♘d5 ♕b8 14 ♗g5 ♖d6 15 ♕a4 h6 16 ♗d2 0-0 17 ♘h4! when White had a powerful initiative. Surprisingly, the Icelandic Grandmaster finished the game by an eventual breakthrough on the queenside: 17 ... ♗c8 18 h3 b5 19 ♘xe7+ ♘xe7 20 ♕c2 ♖fd8 21 ♗e3 c4 22 b4 ♕c7 23 a4 a6 24 axb5 axb5 25 ♖a5 ♕d7 26 ♗c5 ♖d2 27 ♕c1 ♖e8 28 ♖a7 ♕d8 29 ♖xe7! 1-0.

	10	a3	a5
	11	exd5	exd5
	12	♘h4!	

White could fix his opponent's queenside with 12 a4, but Black has compensation in his space advantage. The energetic game move is more in the spirit of the King's Indian Attack.

	12	...	0-0
	13	♘f5	♖e8
	14	♕f3	♕c7
	15	♘f1	♘e5
	16	♕f4!	♗d8 *(40)*

Black defends both the

queen and the king's knight (in case of ♘xh6+), but now Hodgson opens up the black kingside and gains an enduring bind with a piece sacrifice.

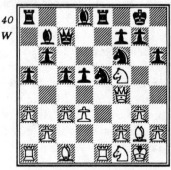

	17	♘xg7!?	♔xg7
	18	♕xh6+	♔g8
	19	♗f4!	♘fg4
	20	♕h5	♖e6
	21	♘e3	♕d7

In a lost position Black tries to give his piece back in the most complicated circumstances possible. 21 ... ♘xe3 22 ♖xe3 ♗f6 23 d4 is a simple win for White.

	22	♘xg4	♘xd3
	23	♘h6+	♔f8
	24	♘f5	♗f6
	25	♗h6+	♔e8 *(41)*

If 25 ... ♔g8 Black gets mated after 26 ♕g4+ ♔h7 27 ♗g7!, threatening 28 ♕h5+ ♔g8 29 ♕h8 mate.

26 ♗g7! ♗xg7

Black ends up a piece down after 26 ... ♔d8 27 ♗xf6+ (27 ... ♖xf6 28 ♕h8+ and 29 ♕xf6).

27 ♖xe6+! 1-0

If 27 ... ♕xe6 28 ♘xg7+ and 29 ♘xe6. Black's queen is also lost after 27 ... ♔d8 28 ♖d6; and in answer to 28 ... ♔f8 White can choose between 29 ♖e7 or 29 ♖h6!?.

Konstantinopolsky – Banas
Correspondence 1985

1	e4	c5
2	♘f3	e6
3	d3	♘c6
4	g3	d5

Remember that if Black holds back the d-pawn then the game would keep its Sicilian character; now we transpose to a French Defence.

5	♘bd2	♘f6
6	♗g2	♗e7
7	0-0	b6
8	♖e1	♗b7
9	e5	*(42)*

White shows that he is happy to follow a more traditional path than waiting with 9 c3 or 9 a3. From this point on the game revolves around the e5–square, which White will over–protect.

9	...	♘d7
10	♘f1	

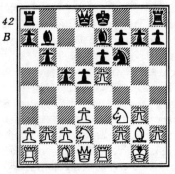

10 c4!? is an interesting alternative, after which White aims to win control of e4 to use as a knight outpost.

The game C. Hansen – Kasparov, Malta Olympiad 1980, went instead 10 h4 ♕c7 11 ♕e2 h6 12 ♘f1 0-0-0 13 ♘1h2 ♖dg8! (an improvement over 13 ... ♔b8, which was seen in Biyiasas – Petrosian, Buenos Aires Olympiad 1978, when 14 ♗f4 ♔a8 15 ♘g4 ♘f8 16 c3 ♘d7 17 a3 b5 18 b4 gave White a slight advantage due to his successful space-gaining initiative on the queenside) 14 ♘g4 ♘f8 15 ♗f4 g5 16 hxg5 hxg5 17 ♗d2 ♖h5 18 c3 ♘g6 19 b4 c4 20 d4 ♖gh8 21 a4 a5 and Black had a comfortable game.

The idea behind 10 ♘f1 is to defend the e-pawn with ♗f4 rather than ♕e2. Consequently, White is able to develop the queen on d2, making Black's ... g7 - g5 break more difficult to realise.

10 ... ♕c7

In Schlenker – Raicevic, Linz 1980, Black opted for 10 ... g5!?, leading to a remarkably complicated battle. There followed 11 ♘e3! h5 (11 ... ♘dxe5 12 ♘xe5 ♘xe5 13 ♘xd5! favours White. Nor does hitting White's knights give Black any joy: 11 ... d4 12 ♘c4 g4 13 ♘g5! - intending ♘e4 - 13 ... ♗xg5 14 ♘d6+) 12 c4 d4 (12 ... g4 13 cxd5! exd5 14 ♘d2 is excellent for White) 13 ♘d5! exd5 14 cxd5 g4 (if 14 ... ♘b4 15 d6 ♗f8 16 ♗xg5) 15 dxc6 ♗xc6 16 e6!! fxe6 17 ♘xd4! ♗xg2 (taking the knight with 17 ... cxd4 is still very good for White - 18 ♗xc6 ♖c8 19 ♖xe6) 18 ♘xe6 ♗f3! 19 ♘xd8! ♗xd1 20 ♘c6 ♖h7 (or 20 ... ♗f3 21 ♖xe7+ ♔f8 22 ♖xd7 ♗xc6 23 ♖c7 with a dangerous initiative) 21 ♗g5 ♗f3 22 ♘xe7 ♔f7 23 ♗h4!, and White had much the better game.

11   ♗f4   0-0-0

The tempting 11 ... g5?! does not work out well for Black here, as 12 ♘xg5 ♘dxe5 13 ♕h5 gives White a clear advantage.

12   h4   h6
13   ♕d2   ♖dg8
14   h5!

A good move. White will not be able to prevent a kingside breakthrough, so he keeps Black temporarily at bay by saddling him with a weak h-pawn after the following advance:

14   ...   g5
15   hxg6   ♖xg6

Better than 15 ... fxg6?! 16 ♗xh6, when Black's g-file will

be blocked and the e-pawn a weakness. In this variation Black finds it easier to have an open g-file and push the h-pawn up the board rather than the other way round, because the ... h5 - h4 thrust threatens to dismantle the white king's pawn cover.

16   ♘e3!

Preparing a pseudo-sacrifice on d5 - a common idea in these positions.

16   ...   h5 (43)

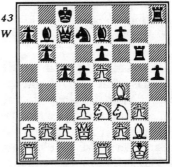

Black judges the threat to be harmless and subsequently continues with his offensive. Indeed, avoiding White's next with 16 ... ♘f8 or 16 ... ♕d8 leaves Black with a passive position.

Challenging the knight is also a faulty plan: 16 ... d4 17 ♘c4 b5 18 ♘d6+ ♗xd6 19 exd6 ♕b6 20 c3! opens up the queenside and gives White a dangerous initiative.

17   ♘xd5!

This pseudo-sacrifice occurs quite often in this line, and the reader should become acquainted with the idea. White clears the e-file for his rook and distracts Black's attention from his kingside attack by putting him on the defensive.

17	...	exd5
18	e6	♛d8

Black prefers to keep his king's bishop on the board so that he can maintain at least some observation of the dark squares on the kingside. Exchanging this piece by 18 ... ♗d6 would merely strengthen White's grip on e5, g5 and (more importantly) h4.

19	exd7+	♛xd7
20	♖xe7!?	

Accentuating the point made in the last note. White considers the enemy bishop to be such an important piece that he is prepared to sacrifice the exchange in order to eliminate it.

Now 20 ... ♘xe7 permits White to win back the exchange in favourable circumstances with 21 ♘e5, although White's activity and raking bishops anyway confer him excellent compensation after the queen recapture.

20	...	♛xe7
21	♗h3+	♖g4

A practical choice, as 21 ... ♔d8 22 ♖e1 ♛f8 (not 22 ... ♛f6 23 ♗g5) 23 ♘h4 leaves Black with two rooks that are no match for the menacing white minor pieces. Note also that his king would be left living dan-

gerously in the centre, cut off on both sides by White's rook and bishops.

22	♖e1	♛d7
23	♘e5?!	

Konstantinopolsky misses his chance to take a clear advantage with 23 d4!, when 23 ... ♖xg3+ 24 ♗xg3 ♛xh3 25 ♛f4 ♛d7 26 ♘e5! ♘xe5 27 ♛xe5 threatens both 28 ♛b8 mate and 28 ♛xh8+. Black now punishes this inaccuracy by playing a pawn to d4 himself, subsequently opening the long diagonal for his hitherto lifeless bishop.

23	...	♘xe5
24	♖xe5	d4!
25	♛e2!	♔d8!

Both sides succeed in finding difficult moves. Again the appealing 25 ... ♖xg3+? fails: 26 fxg3 ♛xh3 27 ♖e8+ ♔d7 28 ♛e7+ ♔c6 29 ♖xh8. Approaching from another angle with 25 ... ♛c6 also proves unsuccessful, since 26 f3! ♛xf3 27 ♖e8+ ♔d7 (27...♖xe8 28 ♛xe8 mate) 28 ♛e7+ ♔c6 29 ♗g2 wins the black queen.

26	♗g5+	♔c8
27	♖e7	(44)
27	...	♛c6?

Ironically, 27 ... ♖xg3+ now draws! The reason is that after 28 fxg3 ♛xh3 29 ♖e8+ ♔d7 30 ♖xh8 ♛h1+ 31 ♔f2 ♛g2+ 32 ♔e1 the queen's bishop no longer defends the g-pawn, making 32 ... ♛xg3+ possible.

Even 30 ♛e7+ does not help

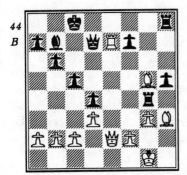

White: 30 ... ♚c6 31 ♖xh8 ♛xg3+ 32 ♔f1 ♛f3+ 33 ♔e1 ♛h1+ 34 ♔d2 ♛g2+ still draws because the retreat 35 ♔e2 leaves the bishop unprotected.

28 ♖xb7!

Removing Black's remaining bishop and ensuring a won game thanks to the power of White's queen and bishops.

28 ...   ♛xb7

28 ... ♚xb7 loses the queen to 29 ♗g2 (29 ... ♛xg2+ 30 ♔xg2 ♖xg5 31 ♛e7+ picks up the greedy rook).

29	f3!	f5
30	fxg4	hxg4
31	♛e5!	

Taking advantage of Black's exposed king to force the rook off the h-file. If now 31 ... ♖xh3 Black loses immediately to 32 ♛e8+ ♔c7 33 ♗f4 mate.

31	...	♖f8
32	♗g2	♛d7
33	♗f4	♔d8

33 ... resigns is an alternative worth consideration. The rest is easy for White.

| 34 | ♛b8+ | ♔e7 |
| 35 | ♗g5+ | ♔f7 |

| 36 | ♛e5 | ♔g6 |
| 37 | ♗e7 | ♖f7 |

Or 37 ... ♖e8 38 ♛f6+ ♔h7 39 ♛f7+ ♔h6 40 ♗g5+ ♔xg5 41 ♛xd7.

38	♗h4	♖f8
39	♗d5	♔h5
40	♗e7	1-0

One finish might be 40 ... ♖c8 41 ♗f7+ ♔h6 42 ♛f6+ ♔h7 43 ♛g6+ ♔h8 44 ♗f6 mate. Remember that Black castled queenside!

Now for a classic example of how not to play the King's Indian Attack. Black reacts to her opponent's passive, stereotyped play by castling queenside and ruthlessly attacking the enemy king.

**Troianska - Jovanovic
Women's Olympiad,
Oberhausen 1966**

1	e4	e6
2	d3	d5
3	♘d2	♘f6
4	♘gf3	c5
5	g3	b6
6	♗g2	♗b7
7	e5	♘fd7
8	0-0	♘c6
9	♖e1	♗e7 (45)
10	c3?	

Too passive. In the above games in which White played an early c3, the e5-push followed only at White's convenience - usually once Black had committed his king. In this game, however, apart from no

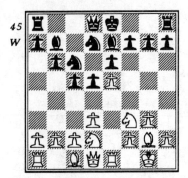

longer having to worry about White advantageously playing exd5, Black already has a target in White's e-pawn.

Consequently, White's best continuation in the diagram position is 10 c4!. The game Jadoul - Kruszynski, Copenhagen 1988, continued 10 ... d4 11 h4 (also possible is Grandmaster Keene's suggestion 11 ♘e4, e.g. 11 ... ♘cxe5 12 ♘xe5 ♘xe5 13 ♘xc5!) 11 ... ♕c7 12 ♘e4! ♘cxe5 13 ♘xe5 ♘xe5 14 ♗f4 0–0 15 ♕h5 f6 16 ♘g5! fxg5 17 ♗xe5 ♕d7 18 hxg5 ♗xg2 19 ♔xg2 with a big advantage to White. Indeed, the pressure on the h-file forced Black to enter into a very passive and inferior ending with 19 ... ♕e8 20 ♕xe8 ♖fxe8 21 f4.

10 ... ♕c7
11 ♕e2

Unfortunately for White defending the e-pawn with 11 d4 does not work. Black can play 11 ... cxd4 12 cxd4 ♘b4 13 ♖e3 ♕c2 14 ♕e1 ♕g6 followed by ... ♘c2.

11 ... g5!

Undermining White's hold on e5 and preparing a kingside attack.

12 h3 0–0–0

Due to the imprecise move order things have not gone well for White. Instead of the usual territorial advantage on the kingside, she is about to face a vigorous offensive on that flank.

13 d4

Jovanovic - Ranniku, Yugoslavia vs USSR 1964, saw White try 13 ♘f1. After 13 ... ♖dg8 14 a3 h5 White prevented ... g5 - g4 by playing 15 g4 first. Black reacted energetically: 15 ... hxg4 16 hxg4 ♗a6 17 ♘g3 ♖h4!! with a crushing attack, as 18 ♘xh4 gxh4 19 ♘f1 ♘cxe5 is much better for Black.

The game move at least 'justifies' 10 c3, but White is not putting any pressure on Black's queenside. Black, on the other hand, embarks on a plan to open up the h-file.

13 ... h5
14 ♘b3 ♖dg8
15 ♘h2 c4
16 ♘d2 g4
17 hxg4

17 h4 keeps the kingside temporarily closed. Then Black may eventually break through with ... ♘d7 - f8 - g6 followed by sacrificing on h4.

17 ... h4! *(46)*

Being a pawn down is irrelevant if Black wants to invade.

18 ♘df1 ♕d8

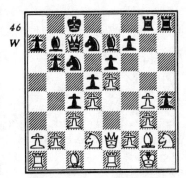

Heading for the kingside.

19	b3	♗a6
20	b4	♕f8
21	a4	♗b7
22	♗f4	hxg3
23	♗xg3	♕h6
24	♘e3	♗g5

Faced with the strong threat of ... ♗f4 White sacrifices.

25	♘xc4	dxc4
26	♕xc4	♗f4

Intending 27 ♗xc6 ♗xg3 28 ♗xb7+ ♔xb7 winning.

27	♘f1	♔b8!
28	♗xc6	

Or 28 ♗xf4 ♕xf4 29 ♗xc6 ♖xg4+.

28	...	♕h1+!! *(47)*

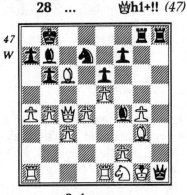

0–1

29 ♗xh1 ♖xh1 is mate. A

fantastic finish, the culmination of very instructive play from Black.

Black Plays ... ♗d6 and ... ♘ge7

Black has also tried keeping watch over the critical e5-square by developing the king's bishop on d6. In combination with ... ♘f6, this would be asking for trouble as White has the dangerous threat of advancing e4 – e5 to fork the two minor pieces. Consequently, e7 is a good square for the knight, when a future ... ♘g6 adds further pressure to e5. To this end, there is also the possibility of ... f6.

The following game provides a good example of how this can work out in practice.

Yudasin – Luther
Leningrad 1989

1	e4	e6
2	d3	d5
3	♘d2	c5
4	♘gf3	♘c6
5	g3	♗d6
6	♗g2	♘ge7 *(48)*

The drawback of Black's set-up is that he is restricted somewhat in flexibility of development, and the lack of influence on e4 in turn gives White more choice of how to continue.

7	0–0	0–0

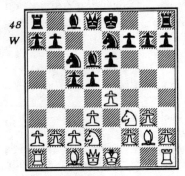

48
W

8   ♖e1

Also possible is 8 ♘h4, followed by 9 f4, as in the game Dolmatov – Lautier, below.

8   ...   ♗c7

Black does not want to be troubled by a future e4 – e5 push, and from c7 the king's bishop may more safely observe e5.

9   c3

Another alternative is 9 exd5 exd5 10 c3, although this would restrict White's choices and unleash the black queen's bishop.

In the game Kaidanov – Motwani, Dublin 1991, White advanced both his wing pawns as far as they could go: 9 h4!? e5 10 exd5 ♘xd5 11 ♘c4 ♗g4 12 c3 ♘b6 13 ♕c2 ♖e8 14 ♘e3 ♗d7 15 a4 h6 16 a5 ♘c8 17 a6 b6 18 h5 with an unclear position. Such a policy as Kaidanov's always runs the risk of wasting four or five moves, after which Black may simply ignore the far-flung pawns and concentrate on play in the centre.

Note that 9 e5? ♘g6 rounds up the e-pawn.

9   ...   d4!?

More sober alternatives are 9 ... b6 and 9 ... f6.

10   ♘b3   b6

10 ... ♗b6? is not at all in keeping with the spirit of the variation, since the bishop will have made several moves to reach this poor square.

11   e5

White does not relish being in a cramped position resulting from ... e6 – e5.

11   ...   ♖b8

The rook must vacate the h1 – a8 diagonal.

12   cxd4   cxd4
13   ♗g5

13 h4 comes to mind, intending h4 – h5 and perhaps even h5 – h6. After 13 ... ♘g6 White could continue 14 h5 ♘gxe5 15 ♘bxd4, or try the more brutal 14 ♘g5 with the idea of 15 ♕h5.

13   ...   ♖e8!

The immediate 13 ... ♗b7 loses the d-pawn after 14 ♗xe7 and 15 ♘bxd4.

14   ♖c1   ♗b7
15   ♖c4!?

An interesting 'waste' of a tempo, putting so much pressure on the enemy d-pawn that Black must create a hole on c5 in order to keep it. White also has a worthy – and probably better – alternative in 15 g4, providing a home for the queen's bishop on the h2 – b8 diagonal after a subsequent

♘f4, over-protecting the e-pawn.

15	**...**	**b5**
16	**♖c1**	**h6!** *(49)*

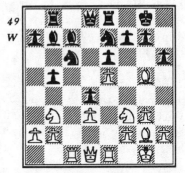

Now 17 ♗xe7 ♖xe7 18 ♘c5 ♗c8 (or 18 ... ♗a8) is slightly better for Black, as is 17 ♘d2 ♘g6 18 ♘c5 ♗c8 19 ♘a6 ♗xa6 20 ♖xc6 ♗b7. White therefore throws down the gauntlet and leaves his bishop on g5.

17 ♘c5!? ♗a8

The passive 17 ... ♗c8 falls in with White's plans: 18 ♘h4! followed by ♕d2 – f4 or queen-side expansion with a3 and b4 is better for White. Incidentally, White need not fear 18 ... g5 as 19 ♗xg5 hxg5 20 ♘xg5 is better for the first player.

18 ♘a6!?

White continues to follow the complicated course. Unwise would be 18 ♗xe7 ♖xe7 19 ♘a6 ♖c8 20 ♘xc7 ♖exc7, leaving all of Black's forces wonderfully placed.

18 ... hxg5!

A risky capture, perhaps, but more promising than 18 ... ♖c8 19 ♘xc7 ♖xc7 20 ♗d2, when

White has a clear advantage thanks to his potentially active – and unchallenged – dark-squared bishop.

19 ♘xg5 g6!

Otherwise 20 ♕h5 signals the end.

20 ♕g4 *(50)*

The game is now reaching boiling point. 20 ♘xb8 would be the first of a sequence of exchanges decisively favourable to White after 20 ... ♕xb8 21 ♕f3 ♘xe5 22 ♕xa8 ♘xd3 23 ♖xc7 ♕xa8 24 ♗xa8 ♘xe1 25 ♖xa7. However, 21 ... ♖f8 should help hold Black's game together, although 22 ♕g4!? does maintain the pressure. This line could be White's best try for advantage, as in the diagram position Black seems to have a saving resource.

20 ... ♗xe5!

The bishop returns to the kingside. After 20 ... ♔g7 White has a number of interesting ways to continue: 21 ♕f4 ♖f8 22 ♘xc7 ♕xc7 23 ♕xf7+!! ♖xf7 24 ♘xe6+ ♔g8 25 ♘xc7 looks good; and 22 ♘xb8 ♕xb8 23

♗xc6!? ♘xc6 24 ♕f6+ ♔g8 25 ♖xc6! ♗xc6 26 ♘xe6! fxe6 27 ♕xg6+ ♔h8 28 ♕h6+ ♔g8 29 ♕xe6+ and 30 ♕xc6 gives White an armada of pawns and an initiative for the piece.

21 ♕h3

White is in danger of trying too hard with 21 ♖xe5, since 21 ... ♘xe5 22 ♕h3 ♗xg2 23 ♕h7+ ♔f8 24 ♕h8+ (24 ♕h6+ is the last chance to draw) 24 ... ♘g8 25 ♕xe5 ♖c8 wins for Black.

21 ... ♗g7

21 ... ♔f8 could be asking for trouble after 22 f4!? ♗g7 23 ♖xe6!? ♖b6! 24 ♘c5.

22 ♘xb8 ♕xb8

23 ♖xe6

White once again powers into his opponent's position, but Black is ready.

23 ... fxe6!

24 ♕xe6+

Not 24 ♕h7+ ♔f8 25 ♘e6+ ♔f7 26 ♕xg7+ ♔xe6 27 ♗h3+ ♔d6 28 ♕f6+ ♔c7, when Black has escaped.

24 ... ♔h8

25 ♕h3+ ½-½

A fitting result to a good spirited and entertaining game.

Dolmatov – Lautier
Poland 1991

1	e4	c5
2	♘f3	e6
3	d3	♘c6
4	g3	d5
5	♘bd2	♗d6
6	♗g2	♘ge7

7	0-0	0-0
8	♘h4!?	

White adopts the hostile plan of pushing the f-pawn which Fischer used to great effect in a crushing victory over Ivkov in 1966 (see below).

8	...	b6
9	f4	dxe4

Black opens the a6 – f1 diagonal so that he can attack White's king's rook and make it awkward for White to support his f-pawn.

10	dxe4	♗a6
11	♖e1	(51)

11 ... ♗c7

In the aforementioned game, Fischer – Ivkov, Santa Monica 1966, Black instead tried 11 ... c4 (with the idea of 12 e5 ♗c5+ 13 ♔h1 c3! 14 bxc3 ♖c8). The rest of this fine game is worth a mention: 12 c3! ♘a5? (better is 12 ... ♖c8, when 13 e5 is met by 13 ... ♗b8) 13 e5 (now the threat of 14 ♗xa8 forces the attacked bishop to leave the important b8 – h2 diagonal and consequently lose its influence on the e5-square) 13 ... ♗c5+ 14 ♔h1

♘d5 15 ♘e4 ♗b7 16 ♕h5! (White should not consider ♘xc5 because a kingside attack holds excellent prospects of netting the full point) 16 ... ♘e7 17 g4! ♗xe4 18 ♗xe4 (the powerful knight has been replaced by a powerful bishop!) 18 ... g6 19 ♕h6 ♘d5 20 f5 ♖e8 (threatening ... ♗f8, but White is too quick) 21 fxg6 fxg6 22 ♘xg6! (winning: 22 ... hxg6 23 ♕xg6+ ♔f8 24 ♖f1+) 22 ... ♕d7 23 ♘f4 and Black did not survive until move 30.

| 12 | c3 | ♗d3 |
| 13 | e5 | ♕d7 |

A way of attempting to justify ... ♗d3 is 13 ... b5!? followed by ... c4, ... ♗c5+ and ... ♘d5. White's next move prevents Black from reverting to this idea.

| 14 | ♘e4! | ♖ad8 |
| 15 | ♕g4 | ♗xe4?! |

White's menacing positions in the King's Indian Attack often tempt Black into 'sacrificing' potentially useful pieces for ostensibly more powerful ones. Such simplification tends to favour White. Allowing the knight to remain on e4 is preferable, parrying the threat of 16 ♘f6+ and 17 ♘xd7 with 15 ... ♔h8.

| 16 | ♗xe4 | ♘g6 |
| 17 | ♘f3 | |

Preparing to jump into g5 at the right moment.

| 17 | ... | ♘ce7 |

Black brings another piece

over to the kingside. Unfortunately for Lautier, his bishop still waits for an opportunity to play a part in the game.

| 18 | ♗c2! | |

A grandmasterly dual-purpose move. The bishop vacates the e4-square - around which White makes his operations - in anticipation of ♘f3 - g5 - e4. Another, equally important, reason behind ♗c2 is that it covers a4. An example of how Black could use this square as an entry point is 18 h4?! ♘f5 19 h5 ♘ge7, threatening the unpleasant ... ♕a4.

18	...	♘f5
19	♘g5	♖fe8
20	♕h5	(52)

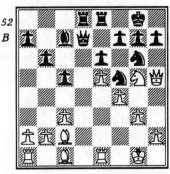

| 20 | ... | ♘h6 |

Offered a difficult choice between this and 20 ... h6, Black decides against the complications which result from hitting the knight: 20 ... h6 21 ♘xe6! ♘xe5! 22 ♕xf5 g6 23 ♕e4 ♖xe6 24 fxe5 ♖xe5 25 ♕xe5 ♗xe5 26 ♖xe5 ♖e8 27 ♖xe8+ ♕xe8 28 ♔f2!, and White's rook and two bishops make too strong a team for the lone queen.

20 ... ♘h6 seems passive, but Black wins time to make a queenside challenge. However, the positioning of the respective forces indicates that White is in no hurry to break into his opponent's kingside.

21	h4	b5
22	♔h2	b4
23	♕e2	♘f5
24	h5	♘f8
25	♘e4!	♕c6
26	g4	♘e7

Black can do nothing but wait for the charge.

27 h6!

Underlining the vulnerability of Black's f6-square. Note that the area around Black's king is the part of the board on which the action takes place, yet the black pieces have no significant influence there.

27	...	♘d7
28	hxg7	♔xg7
29	♔g3!	

Threatening simply to invade down the h-file.

29	...	♘g6
30	♗e3?	

This permits Black to strike out in the centre and activate his pieces with a sacrifice that breaks White's grip. White should keep the chains in place by 30 g5, and only then continue with his plan to transfer to the h-file.

30	...	bxc3
31	bxc3	♘dxe5! *(53)*

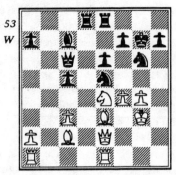

32	fxe5	♗xe5+
33	♔h3!	f5!

If 30 g5 had been played instead of 30 ♗e3 the sacrifice would be much less potent, since now White would be able to play 34 gxf6+.

34	♘g3	♔h8
35	♘h5	♗xc3?

35 ... ♖g8!? is an interesting alternative, when Black has pressure down the g-file. It is understandable that Black seeks to regain material, but he risks returning the initiative.

36	♗g5!	♖b8
37	♖ab1	♕xe1
38	♖xe1	c4
39	♗f6+	♔g8
40	♗c3!	

White's minor pieces are too powerful.

40	...	♔f7
41	♖f1	♕c5
42	♕d2!	

After the scare caused by 30 ♗e3?, White is once again in command. The immediate threat is ♕h6, but all of White's pieces are aimed at the enemy king. It is impossible for Black to defend.

42	...	♕e7
43	♗xf5!	♕h4+

Or 43 ... exf5 44 ♖xf5+ ♔g8 45 ♕d5+ ♕e6 46 ♘f6+.

44	♔g2	♖bd8
45	♗xe6+!	♔e7
46	♗b4+	1-0

Black cannot escape the crossfire: 46 ... ♔xe6 47 ♘g7+ ♔e5 48 ♗c3+.

Black Plays An Early ... dxe4

Finally, a game in which Black follows a recommendation given in several books about the French Defence - the immediate central pawn exchange. It is true that White's advantage is slight, but the positions are very similar to others which arise from the King's Indian Attack, and White tends to have more attractive squares for his pieces.

Belkhodja - Crouch
Cappelle la Grande 1991

1	e4	e6
2	d3	d5
3	♘d2	♘f6
4	g3	

Perhaps a more accurate move order is 4 ♘gf3 when after 4 ... dxe4 5 dxe4, a routine and premature capture, White has the opportunity to develop his king's bishop on d3.

The game Ree - Pederson, Groningen 1965/66, continued 5 ... ♗c5 6 ♗d3 b6 7 ♕e2 ♗b7 8 0-0 ♘bd7 9 c3 ♗e7 10 e5 ♘d5 11 ♘e4 c5? 12 ♘g5! and Black was in trouble.

4	...	dxe4
5	dxe4	♘c6
6	♗g2	♗c5
7	♘gf3	e5 *(54)*

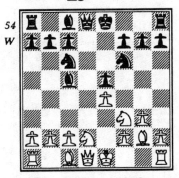

It is imperative that Black prevent White's space-gaining b2 - b4 advance.

10 ♕c2

Defending the e-pawn in preparation for ♘c4.

10	...	♗d6?!
11	♘g5?!	

White returns the favour by replying to Black's strange tenth move with an equally useless one. It seems from what happens later that White is trying to tempt ... h7 - h6. More fitting is 11 a4 or 11 h3.

11	...	♗g4
12	♘c4	♗h5
13	♘f3	♖e8
14	♗g5	h6

8	0-0	0-0
9	c3	a5!

15 ♗e3

White calculates that the tempo spent in enticing ... h6 will prove to be a worthy investment when a knight arrives on f5, as hitting the knight with ... g6 would then lose the h6-pawn.

15	...	♗f8
16	♖ad1	♛c8
17	a4	♛e6
18	b3	♖ad8 *(55)*

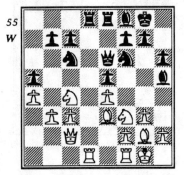

White has a nagging edge which he hopes to make more tangible by trading off into an ending. Until then, he also has a grip on the light squares and a pull on the kingside thanks to the availability of the f5-square.

19	♖xd8	♖xd8
20	♘h4	♛d7
21	f3	g5
22	♘f5	♗g6
23	♗h3	

White wants to maintain a piece on f5.

23	...	♛d3
24	♛xd3	♖xd3
25	♖c1	

Black's active rook is soon to be evicted.

25	...	♘e8
26	♔f2	f6

Providing the queen's bishop with a route back into the game.

27	♔e2	♖d8
28	♗f2	

Although White has played the entire game without making any particularly serious threats, his positional handling has been excellent. Black has also fared well, but he still finds himself defending weak squares on d5 and f5.

28	...	♗f7
29	♘fe3	♗c5
30	♘d5!	

White takes advantage of a tactic to further his positional superiority. Now 30 ... ♗xf2 31 ♔xf2 ♗xd5? 32 exd5 wins a pawn for White because 32 ... ♖xd5 fails to 33 ♗e6+ and ♗xd5.

30	...	♗xf2
31	♔xf2	♔f8
32	♘ce3	♘e7
33	c4	♘g8

Exchanging on d5 will leave White with a strong pawn there whichever way he recaptures. The point of Black's move is to defend the h6-pawn (which White tempted forward as early as the fourteenth move!) against a possible ♘f5.

34 ♔e2

Keeping guard over d3 in anticipation of Black's next.

34	...	c6
35	♘b6	♔e7
36	c5!? *(56)*	

An interesting winning try.

White sacrifices a pawn in return for pressure against Black's a- and b-pawns. If Black declines White will anyway attack the a-pawn with ♘ec4.

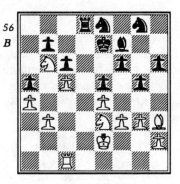

36	...	♗xb3
37	♖b1	♗a2
38	♖b2	♗e6
39	♗xe6	♔xe6
40	♘bc4	

Winning back his pawn with a decisive advantage. White has a dominating position.

| 40 | ... | ♘e7 |
| 41 | ♖xb7 | f5 |

Black endeavours to break White's grip, but this does not change the final outcome:

42	exf5+	♘xf5
43	♘xf5	♔xf5
44	♘xa5	e4
45	fxe4+	♔xe4
46	♘xc6	♖a8
47	♘a7	♔d5
48	c6	♘d6
49	♖d7	♔c5
50	a5	♘c8
51	♘xc8	♖xc8
52	c7	♔b5
53	♔f3	♔xa5
54	♔g4	1-0

A textbook-like positional display from the French International Master, showing the reader how calm, controlled methods can be used against Black's equalising attempt.

4 KIA vs Caro-Kann Defence

1	e4	c6
2	d3	*(57)*

Before looking at the more popular ways of meeting 2 d3, it must be noted that Black has an uncompromising line which threatens to take the initiative should White continue in a stereotyped fashion:

2	...	d5
3	♘d2	dxe4
4	dxe4	e5
5	♘gf3	♗c5

Black ignores the threat to his e-pawn because he intends to meet 6 ♘xe5 with 6 ... ♗xf2+ (defending with 5 ... ♕c7 grants White a commanding position after 6 ♘c4 - also possible is 6 ♗c4 - 6 ... ♘d7 7 a4 ♘gf6 8 ♗d3). If White dare not take up the challenge Black can develop

his pieces freely, so the only way to strive for an advantage is to follow Grandmaster Raymond Keene's advice and strike immediately:

6	♘xe5!	♗xf2+
7	♔xf2	♕d4+
8	♔e1	♕xe5
9	♘c4!	*(58)*

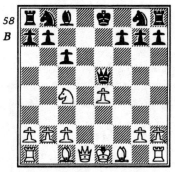

The point. It is true that White can no longer castle, but Black is very weak on the dark squares now that he has given White the advantage of the two bishops, and the unpleasant threat of ♘d6+ more or less forces Black's hand:

9	...	♕xe4+
10	♗e2	

Now 10 ... ♕xg2 11 ♘d6+ ♔f8 12 ♖f1 ♗e6 13 ♘xf7! wins due to 13 ... ♗xf7 14 ♕d8 mate. This leads us to 10 ... ♕e6 11 ♘d6+ ♔e7 12 ♘xc8+ ♕xc8 13 ♕d4! with a tremendous position for White. An interesting alternative is 10 ♔f2, when a future ♖e1 will cause Black problems.

Black has two main continuations against 2 d3, distinguished by where the king's bishop will go. One idea is to follow White's example and support the centre with a kingside fianchetto, following up with ... e5 and ... ♘e7 or simply developing with ... ♘f6 and omitting ... e5. Karpov once opted for ... e5, ... ♘f6 and ... d6 instead, but White then has a free hand on the queenside (see Ljubojevic – Karpov). Another way of maintaining pawns on d5 and e5 is by playing ... ♗d6, ... ♘f6 and ... ♖e8, as in Anand – Malaniuk.

A less ambitious policy which 'quiet' opponents may prefer involves holding back the e-pawn altogether and making the central exchange ... dxe4. The resulting symmetrical pawn structure works out in White's favour as the extra move and territorial superiority afford White the better game.

Black Fianchettoes Kingside

Wojtkiewicz – Bronstein
Polanica Zdroj 1988

1	e4	c6
2	d3	d5
3	♘d2	g6

4	♘gf3	♗g7
5	g3	e5
6	♗g2	♘e7

By playing ... e5 and ... ♘e7 Black takes a share of the central territory and puts a stop to White's space-gaining e4 – e5 push.

7	0-0	0-0	(59)

8 ♖e1

A popular continuation for White is to play b2 – b4 here, or on the next move, to take advantage of Black's decision to voluntarily close his king's bishop's long a1 – h8 diagonal. Ermolinsky – Tukmakov, Sverdlovsk 1987, continued 8 b4 a5 9 bxa5 ♕xa5 10 ♗b2 d4 11 a4 (better than 11 ♕c1?!, which was played in Short – Miles, Wijk aan Zee 1987 as after 11 ... ♘d7 12 ♘b3 ♕a4! Black had used White's omission of a2 – a4 to steal the advantage) 11 ... ♕c7 12 c3 dxc3 13 ♗xc3 c5 14 ♘c4 ♘ec6 15 ♕b3 ♘a6 16 ♘b6 with a slight pull for White.

In the game Maier – Muse, West Germany 1987, White (after 8 b4 a5) ignored the threat to his b-pawn and hit the black e-pawn with 9 ♗b2!?. For some reason, Black decided against the obvious and punishing 9 ... axb4, going for the safer 9 ... ♘d7 10 a3 ♕c7 11 d4 exd4 12 ♗xd4 ♗xd4 13 ♘xd4 with a roughly equal position. The continuation 8 c3 ♘d7 9 b4 is discussed in the next game (Stein – Hort).

It is purely a matter of taste whether or not White goes for immediate expansion on the queenside or – as in this game – continue with central development, threatening to win the e-pawn after first exchanging on d5.

> **8 ... d4**

Black closes the centre. After 8 ... ♘d7 White might return to the idea mentioned in the last note by playing 9 b4.

> **9 ♘c4!? b5**

Bronstein answers White's provocative play by accepting the invitation to march his pawns down the board. White cannot take the e-pawn now because after 10 ♘cxe5 f6 wins a piece.

> **10 ♘cd2 c5**
> **11 a4!**

Part of the plan. White gave away a couple of moves in order to lure the enemy pawns forward and subsequently take control of the c4-square.

> **11 ... b4**
> **12 ♘c4 ♘d7**
> **13 ♘fd2**

Clearing the way for the f-pawn now that Black's counterplay on the other wing has been nipped in the bud.

> **13 ... ♘b6**
> **14 f4!**

White begins to attack on the kingside.

> **14 ... f6**

Black bolsters his e-pawn, waiting until the time is right before playing ... exf4.

> **15 ♖f1 ♖b8**

Another preparatory move which is quite common in the King's Indian Attack. Black moves his rook out of the firing line of White's king's bishop in anticipation of the coming ... exf4.

> **16 ♘f3 ♘xc4**
> **17 dxc4** *(60)*

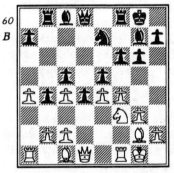

White must have judged the exchange of his well-posted knight as not detrimental to his game. Furthermore, the newly-arrived c4-pawn will help blockade the queenside.

> **17 ... exf4**
> **18 gxf4 ♗g4**

Preventing the useful knight

manoeuvre ♘f3 – e1 – d3.

19	b3	♖e8

Bronstein gives White something to think about by intending to attack the e-pawn.

20	h3	♗h5
21	♕d3	

Escaping the pin and defending the e-pawn.

21	...	♘c8
22	♗d2	♖b7
23	♖ae1	♖be7

Black has organised his forces well considering his difficulties in the transition between opening and middlegame. Nevertheless, White still has an initiative and, because Black had to bring pieces to cover the kingside, a better game on both sides of the board (Black's queenside pawns are permanently weak).

24	e5!?	

A speculative advance which aims to break into Black's camp. Now 24 ... fxe5 25 ♘xe5 ♗xe5 26 fxe5 ♖xe5 27 ♖xe5 ♖xe5 28 ♗h6 gives White excellent compensation for the sacrificed pawn, e.g. 28 ... ♗e2 29 ♕g3 ♖e8 30 ♗d5+ ♔h8 31 ♖f7. Alternatively, 24 ... ♗xf3 25 ♗xf3 fxe5 26 f5!? leaves Black very weak on the light squares, not forgetting White's much superior pieces. Therefore Bronstein prefers to keep his position as stable as possible.

24	...	♘b6
25	exf6	♗xf6
26	♖xe7	♖xe7

27	♖e1	

White considers that he can exchange all the rooks and still retain good attacking chances.

27	...	♖xe1+
28	♘xe1	♕e7
29	♘f3	

White has good enough command of the light squares even without his king's bishop. Black's problem now is his weak c-pawn, as White is about to realise the plan of transferring a knight to d3. Remember that Black interfered with this sortie with his 18th move.

29	...	♗xf3
30	♕xf3	(61)

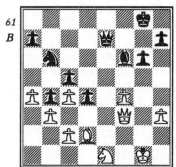

61
B

Unfortunately for Black, the arrival of an ending has not rid him of his defensive task.

30	...	♕e6

Improving the position of the queen and preparing to defend the c-pawn with a less powerful piece.

31	♘d3	♗e7
32	♘e5	a6
33	♕b7	♘c8
34	♔g2	♔g7

35 a5 g5

Black tries to break out of his restraints, so White decides it is time to offer a trade of queens.

36 ♕d5 ♕f5
37 ♘d3 ♕xd5+
38 cxd5 h6

Or 38 ... gxf4 39 ♗xf4, with the idea of ♗f4 - c7 - b6. Consequently, Black prefers to keep the bishop locked out.

39 ♔f3 ♔g6
40 fxg5 hxg5

40 ... ♗xg5 leaves the c-pawn undefended.

41 ♔g4 1-0

Black resigned because either the c-pawn or the g-pawn (perhaps even both) will fall. One threat is 42 ♘e5+.

Stein - Hort
Los Angeles 1968

1 e4 c6
2 d3 d5
3 ♘d2 g6
4 g3 ♗g7
5 ♗g2 e5
6 ♘gf3 ♘e7

6 ... ♘h6?! neglects the centre and was rightly punished in Ribli - Barcza, Budapest 1971. The game continued 7 0-0 0-0 8 exd5! (Stein - Barcza, Caracas 1970, went 8 b4 f6 9 ♘b3 dxe4 10 dxe4 ♕xd1 11 ♖xd1 b6 12 ♗f1 ♘f7 13 ♗e3 ♗g4 14 ♔g2 ♘d7 15 h3 ♗e6? 16 ♘bd4!! exd4 17 ♘xd4 f5 18 ♘xe6 ♗xa1 19 ♘xf8 ♘xf8 20 ♖xa1 fxe4 21 a4! with a clear plus for White) 8 ... cxd5 9 c4 ♘c6 10 cxd5 ♕xd5 11 ♘c4 ♕e6 12 ♗xh6! ♗xh6 13 ♘fxe5! ♘xe5 14 ♖e1 f6 15 f4 and White had a very active game.

7 0-0 0-0
8 c3 ♘d7
9 b4! b6
10 ♗b2 ♗b7
11 ♖e1 ♖e8
12 ♗h3 (62)

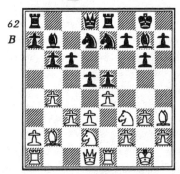

Over the last few moves White has been indirectly attacking the e5-pawn. Black now decides to offer a sacrifice rather than remain on the defensive.

12 ... ♕c7!?
13 exd5 cxd5
14 c4!

A good choice. After 14 ♗xd7 ♕xd7 15 ♘xe5 ♕xe5 16 ♖xe5 ♘c6 17 ♖xe8+ ♖xe8 Black would have excellent compensation for the pawn by playing against White's light-square weaknesses. The game continuation, however, helps White maintain an advantage by granting him a dangerous pawn majority on the queenside.

14 ...   d4

Not 14 ... dxc4? 15 ♘xc4 when Black's weak e-pawn will cause him serious strategical problems.

15 ♖c1   f5

Black must also attempt to roll his pawns down the board.

16 ♗g2   ♗f6

Denying White access to e6, e.g. 16 ... ♕d6? 17 ♕b3 ♕e6 18 ♘g5!.

17 c5!

Helped by the threat to win material with 18 c6! (18 ... ♘xc6 19 b5), White forces either a supported passed pawn or a favourable opening up of the position.

17 ...   b5

The lesser evil, as 17 ... bxc5 18 bxc5 ♗d5 (not 18 ... ♘xc5 19 ♘b3) 19 ♘c4 gives Black another unpleasant choice – to relinquish the bishop pair or allow ♘d6 (note that 19 ... ♘c8 is met by 20 ♘xd4 when 20 ... exd4 loses the now undefended rook on e8).

18 ♘b3

Intending an occupation of a5 in the near future.

18 ...   ♗d5

19 a4!

Now after 19 ... bxa4 20 ♘a5 White will follow up the recapture of the front a-pawn with an attack on its remaining partner on a7. Black opts to saddle himself with a weak b-pawn instead.

19 ...   a6

20 ♘a5   ♘c6

Black thematically blocks the path of the passed pawn, but perhaps better was 20 ... ♔g7, with a great game for White.

21 axb5

Also good is 21 ♘xe5! ♖xe5 22 ♗xd5+ ♖xd5 23 ♕b3 ♘xb4 24 ♗a3!, but Stein's way of playing the combination is more pleasing.

21 ...   axb5

22 ♘xe5!! *(63)*

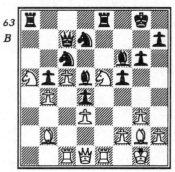

22 ...   ♘xb4

As in the last note, 22 ... ♖xe5 23 ♗xd5+ ♖xd5 24 ♕b3 ♘xb4 25 ♗a3! looks very good for White. Another interesting move is 24 ♕f3!?.

23 ♘xd7   ♕xd7

24 c6!

White's brave c-pawn marches on.

24 ...   ♕f7

25 ♖xe8+   ♖xe8

26 ♘b7!

Threatening to win the exchange with ♘d6.

26 ...   ♗e5

27 ♗xd5   ♕xd5

28 ♖c5 ♕f7

28 ... ♕e6 29 c7 is crushing, e.g. 29 ... ♖c8 30 ♕e2.

29 ♕f3 g5?!

Ambitious, although after the better 29 ... ♘a6 30 ♖xb5 ♘c7 31 ♖b4 White is winning.

30 c7! g4

Because of Black's twenty-ninth move, 30 ... ♗xc7 allows 31 ♖xf5. Now Black does succeed in winning the c-pawn, but White has switched his attentions to a kingside attack.

31 ♕d1 ♗xc7
32 ♕d2 ♗b6

32 ... ♗e5 offers more hope of prolonging the game. Now White goes on the warpath.

33 ♖xb5 ♘xd3

Against 33 ... ♕xb7 the best reply is 34 ♖xb4!, not 34 ♕xb4?? ♕f3! with a draw! Now, despite being in time-trouble, White skilfully paves his way through the complications to emerge with a won game.

34 ♘d6 ♕d7
35 ♕g5+ ♔h8
36 ♕f6+ ♔g8
37 ♕g5+ ♔h8
38 ♘xe8! ♕xe8
39 ♕xf5

Unfortunately for Black, Stein's last defends against 39 ... ♕e1+ 40 ♔g2 ♕xf2+.

39 ... ♘e5
40 ♖xb6 ♘f3+
41 ♔g2!

Even now White must be careful – 41 ♔f1?? ♕e1+ 42 ♔g2 ♕g1 mate.

41 ... ♕a8

Black could resign here.

42 ♕f6+ ♔g8
43 ♕e6+ ♔h8

Or 43 ... ♔f8 44 ♘a3+ ♕xa3 45 ♖b8+ ♔g7 46 ♖g8 mate.

43 ♕c6 1-0

Fischer – Ibrahimoglu
Siegen Olympiad 1970

1	e4	c6
2	d3	d5
3	♘d2	g6
4	♘gf3	♗g7
5	g3	♘f6

Instead of spending time with 5 ... e5 and 6 ... ♘e7, Black develops simply. This plan is less ambitious than forming a pawn centre, and White is guaranteed a slight edge.

6	♗g2	0-0
7	0-0	♗g4 (64)

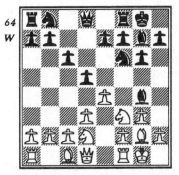

Black develops his 'problem piece'. The alternative 7 ... dxe4 transposes to the next game.

8 h3

Also possible is 8 ♖e1, as Black's last move intends to concede the bishop pair in any case.

8	...	♗xf3
9	♕xf3	♘bd7
10	♕e2	dxe4
11	dxe4	♕c7

White was threatening 12 e5 followed by 13 e6!, opening the e-file and weakening Black's light squares.

12 a4

This is the first stage of a plan designed to attack Black's queenside. White gains space and prepares to either tie Black down to the defence of the a-pawn or force positional concessions.

| 12 | ... | ♖ad8 |
| 13 | ♘b3 | b6 |

Black had to do something about Fischer's next move. 13 ... a5 leaves the queenside pawns weak and susceptible to attack from now until the endgame; whilst 13 ... a6 is also an un-attractive move to make, as 14 a5! eyes the hole on b6 and fixes the queenside. Were Black to eventually play ... b5, White could then capture en passant with axb6, thus saddling Black with a very weak a-pawn.

14 ♗e3 c5

After this advance White's pieces are denied the use of d4 and his queen's bishop no longer pressures b6. Black can also avoid the splitting of his queenside pawns. Nevertheless, one of the Golden Rules of chess – which is often not fully appreciated – advises that "every pawn move automatic-ally creates a weakness." In this case the new hole on b5 helps White stay on top.

15 a5 e5

Black prevents a future f4 and e5.

16 ♘d2 ♘e8!

Heading for c7 to defend the white squares on the queenside.

17 axb6 axb6 *(65)*

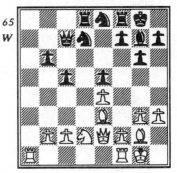

18 ♘b1!

White's knight takes up the challenge to control b5 by reaching there via b1. Black prepares for the invasion.

18	...	♕b7
19	♘c3	♘c7
20	♘b5	♕c6

Both avoiding 21 ♖a7 and forcing White to exchange his troublesome knight.

| 21 | ♘xc7 | ♕xc7 |
| 22 | ♕b5! | |

Otherwise Black will play 22 ... ♕c6, when White only has a small edge. Now Fischer persists with his queenside pressure, concentrating on Black's b-pawn. His play on the light squares is instructive – and Black never gets the time to counter-attack.

22	...	♖a8
23	c3	♖xa1
24	♖xa1	♖b8

A dual-purpose move which defends the b-pawn and prepares - if possible - to exchange the final pair of rooks with ... ♖b8 - b7 - a7.

| 25 | ♖a6 | ♗f8 |
| 26 | ♗f1! | |

White accentuates his domination of the queenside by strengthening the f1 - a6 diagonal, also relieving the queen of her duties on b5.

26	...	♔g7
27	♕a4	♖b7
28	♗b5!	

Fischer crowns his accurate positional punishment of Black's fourteenth move with the threat of 29 ♗xd7 ♕xd7 30 ♕xd7 ♖xd7 31 ♖xb6. Thus Black is forced into a horribly passive position.

| 28 | ... | ♘b8 |

Unfortunately for Black, 28 ... ♘f6 allows 29 ♗c6 ♖b8 30 ♖a7 with pressure on the seventh rank.

| 29 | ♖a8 | ♗d6 |
| 30 | ♕d1! | |

Highlighting the power of White's pieces. His rook – helped by the king's bishop – is the master of the queenside; his queen enjoys great freedom of movement; and now even the remaining bishop is about to play its part. It is important to note that White's last move does not permit his opponent to relieve the pressure with 30 ... ♖a7 as 31 ♖xa7 ♕xa7 32 ♕xd6 wins a piece. In the meantime, the black pieces are huddled together on the queenside, so he sets about unravelling them.

| 30 | ... | ♘c6 |
| 31 | ♕d2! | h5 |

Vacating h7 for the king. Not 31 ... ♖b8? 32 ♘h6+ ♔g8 33 ♗xc6! ♕xc6 34 ♖xb8+ ♗xb8 35 ♕d8+; or 32 ... ♔f6 33 ♕g5+ ♔e6 34 ♖xb8 and 35 ♗c4+.

| 32 | ♘h6+ | ♔h7 |
| 33 | ♗g5 | |

Threatening 34 ♗f6.

33	...	♖b8
34	♖xb8	♘xb8
35	♗f6!	

White's invasion is almost complete. He still has three active pieces compared with Black's 'spectators'.

| 35 | ... | ♘c6 |

Not 35 ... ♘d7? 36 ♗xd7 ♕xd7 37 ♗xe5.

| 36 | ♕d5 | ♘a7 |

If 36 ... ♘d8 37 ♗xd8 ♕xd8 38 ♕xf7+.

| 37 | ♗e8! | |

The winning move. Black's position is overloaded.

37	...	♔g8
38	♗xf7+	♕xf7
39	♕xd6	1-0

Balashov – Tisdall
Reykjavik 1989

| 1 | e4 | c6 |

2	d3	d5
3	♘d2	g6
4	♘gf3	♗g7
5	g3	dxe4

A committal but solid continuation. White no longer has to worry about his opponent creating complications in the near future after this simplifying central exchange.

6	dxe4	♘f6
7	♗g2	0-0
8	0-0	♘a6 *(66)*

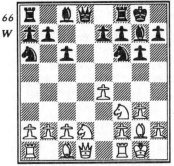

Caro-Kann players often have problems developing the queenside minor pieces when faced with the King's Indian Attack, particularly the queen's bishop (in the previous game Black traded it off at the earliest opportunity). This drawback and the symmetrical nature of the pawn structure give White a persistent and safe advantage.

The game Bagirov - Scherbakov, Budapest 1989, continued 8 ... ♘bd7 9 e5! ♘d5 10 e6!, disrupting Black's pawns. After 10 ... fxe6 11 ♕e2 ♔h8 12 ♘g5! (White loses his queen after 12 ♕xe6?? ♘e5!) 12 ... ♘c7 13 ♘df3

e5 14 ♕c4 e4 15 ♕xe4 ♘f6 16 ♕h4 ♘e6 17 ♖e1 ♘xg5 18 ♗xg5 White was well on top.

| 9 | ♕e2 |

9 e5 was seen in Stein - Portisch, Moscow 1967, with White retaining a slight pull in the middlegame after 9 ... ♘d5 10 ♘b3 ♗g4 11 ♕e2 ♕c8 12 ♖e1 ♘ac7 13 ♗d2 f6 14 exf6 ♗xf6 15 c3 ♖f7 16 ♕e4 ♗f5 17 ♕c4 ♘b6 18 ♕f1 ♘a4 19 ♗c1 ♕d7 20 ♘e5 ♗xe5 21 ♖xe5. Balashov prefers to wait for Black to show his hand before pushing the e-pawn.

| 9 | ... | ♕a5 |
| 10 | e5 |

Black may have been toying with the idea of transferring his queen over to the kingside with ... ♕h5, so this must have helped White decide to make this space-gaining move. The attacked knight will now be chased across the board to join its passive partner.

| 10 | ... | ♘d5 |

The best square. 10 ... ♘e8 looks ugly and 10 ... ♘d7 11 e6 saddles Black with a weak e-pawn.

| 11 | ♘b3 | ♕c7 |
| 12 | c4 |

Staking a claim to central territory and simultaneously putting the question to the knight. Now 12 ... ♘db4 13 a3 wins for White, so Black's next is forced.

| 12 | ... | ♘b6 |
| 13 | ♗f4 |

White introduces the threat of 14 e6 by lining the bishop up with the enemy queen.

13 ... ♗e6

Usefully blocking while developing. Black also threatens the c-pawn and prepares to bring a rook to the d-file.

14 ♖ac1 ♖ad8
15 ♘bd4

Now that White's forces are harmoniously placed he adds pressure to the e6-square. If he is allowed a timely ♘xe6 then Black will be left with a couple of weak e-pawns and no promise of freeing his king's bishop with ... f7 - f6.

15 ... ♗g4

Inviting the thrust e5 - e6, although with a more active game than a few moves ago Black would no longer be troubled so much by this push. Now Black has a somewhat cramped position so White elects to take an advantage in the form of the bishop pair, more space and excellent chances of engineering a kingside attack.

16 h3 ♗xf3

Such an exchange helps relieve the pressure on the defender and is better than dropping the bishop back to c8, whence it would have a future with few prospects.

17 ♘xf3 e6
18 b3 h6
19 h4

All three of White's minor pieces are ready to begin action on the kingside. As for Black, his knights are at the moment lacking any significant influence on the game, and if he does not act quickly in the centre or on the queenside, then White will be left to build up threats against the black king.

19 ... ♘b4

Black correctly begins his diversionary tactics. The immediate threat is to jump in with ... ♘d3, which explains White's next.

20 ♖c3 c5

Improving his position further. Suddenly, the queen's knight is heading (via c6) for d4.

21 ♖e1 ♖d7
22 a3

It is true that White seems to be helping the knight's invasion, but with the queen tied to the defence of the a-pawn it is not possible to pressurise the black h-pawn and concentrate fire-power on the kingside.

22 ... ♘c6
23 ♕e3 ♘d4 (67)

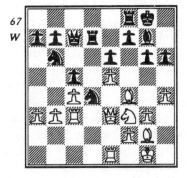

67
W

Black has accomplished his aim. Even 24 ♗xh6? is now ruled out thanks to 24 ... ♘f5. We have reached the point of the game in which White must accelerate the pace or relinquish his initiative. Balashov is up to the task.

24 g4!

Unlike many openings, the King's Indian Attack offers White a very good opportunity of troubling the enemy king (especially with such a pawn advance), often without fear of a dangerous counter-attack in another sector of the board. Apart from intending h4 - h5, White's aggressive move also deprives Black the use of the f5-square.

24 ...   ♔h7

In view of what follows, it may have been a good idea to play 24 ... ♘xf3+, although White would still be able to use e4 for his king's bishop. But exchanging knights is a difficult decision to arrive at when one considers the number of moves Black invested to establish the outpost on d4.

25 ♘d2

White prepares to transfer his knight to e4, ignoring its ostensibly powerful counterpart.

25 ...   ♖c8

Black's weak f6-square needs covering, so in anticipation of the arrival of a knight on e4 Black releases his queen

from the defence of the c-pawn.

26 ♘e4   ♕d8
27 ♘f6+

The first strike. Moving the king not only loses the h-pawn, but leaves the knight firmly entrenched in the black camp, hence his choice.

27 ...   ♗xf6
28 exf6   h5

With all of Black's pieces on the queenside, a successful breakthrough from White is inevitable if Black follows a sit and wait policy.

29 gxh5   ♕xf6
30 ♗e5   ♕xh4
31 hxg6+   fxg6 *(68)*

32 ♕c1!

A wonderful move with which White secures victory. The queen clears the way for the queen's rook to come to the h-file.

32 ...   ♕g4
33 ♖h3+   ♔g8
34 ♕h6   1-0

This time the white queen makes the final threat – that of 35 ♕h8+ ♔f7 36 ♖h7 mate.

Unfortunately for Black, there is no adequate defence.

Ljubojevic – Karpov
Amsterdam 1988

1	e4	c6
2	d3	e5!?
3	♘d2	♘f6
4	♘gf3	d6

When Black refrains from playing an early ... d5 the lack of tension in the centre makes it easier for both sides to concentrate on development. White usually takes advantage of this by gaining space on the queenside.

5	g3	g6

Developing the bishop on e7 is also possible, but not as active as the fianchetto.

6	♗g2	♗g7
7	0–0	0–0
8	a4	♘bd7
9	a5!	♖e8
10	b4	♖b8
11	♗b2	*(69)*

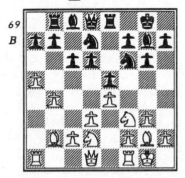

Black is in danger of being overrun on the queenside, so the ex-World Champion grants White the a-file in return for development of the queen's bishop and a future challenge with ... ♖a8.

11	...	b5
12	axb6	

The only way for White to play for an advantage. Against other moves Black would continue ... a6, ... ♗b7 and ... c5 or ... d5.

12	...	axb6
13	♖a7	♗b7
14	c4	♕c7
15	♕b3	♖a8
16	♖xa8	♗xa8
17	♖a1	d5?!

Understandably, Black must have felt uncomfortably cramped, but a preparatory move such as 17 ... h6 was better if Black wanted to break out with ... d5.

18	cxd5	cxd5
19	♘g5!	♕d6

In the event of 19 ... h6 White can secure a safe advantage after 20 exd5 hxg5 21 d6 ♕xd6 22 ♗xa8, or enter into complications with 20 ♘xf7! ♔xf7 21 exd5 ♕d6 (or 21 ... ♔f8 22 d6! followed by ♗xa8) 22 ♘c4.

20	exd5	♗xd5

Not 20 ... ♘xd5? 21 ♖xa8 ♖xa8 22 ♗xd5 with a won game for White.

21	♘c4!	♕c6
22	♘e3!	*(70)*

White catches his opponent in the criss-cross of diagonals. Now 22 ... ♗xg2 is met with 23 ♕xf7+ ♔h8 24 ♘xg2, so Black has no choice but to exchange queens, after which White is much better.

22	...	♗xb3
23	♗xc6	h6
24	♖a3!	hxg5
25	♖xb3	

In many variations of the King's Indian Attack, White's build-up of pressure results in his winning the bishop pair. Once this is achieved, White's initiative should then be sufficient to extract further gains. Black's task now is to transfer his bishop from 'g7' to the vulnerable queenside.

25	...	♗f8
26	♔g2	♖e6
27	♗b5	♔g7
28	h3	♗e7
29	♗c3	

Ljubojevic frees his rook from the defence of the b-pawn, so as to regain control of the a-file.

29	...	♗d6
30	♖a3	♗b8
31	♖a8	♖e7
32	♗d2!	

Intending 33 ♘c4, hitting the

g-pawn and threatening 34 ♘xb6 ♘xb6 35 ♖xb8. Apart from being in a terrible position, Black was also quite short of time.

32	...	e4
33	d4	♗c7
34	♖c8	♘f8
35	♗c3	♘8h7

Not 35 ... ♘e6 36 d5.

| 36 | ♗c6 | ♘f8 |
| 37 | b5 *(71)* | 1-0 |

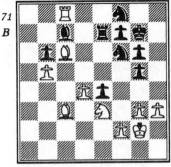

Black lost on time here, but a brief examination of the position shows us that White is winning.

Black Plays ... ♗d6

In the following game Black does not fianchetto his king's bishop but supports his central advances in another fashion.

Anand – Malaniuk
Frunze 1987

1	e4	c6
2	d3	d5
3	♘d2	e5
4	♘gf3	♗d6 *(72)*

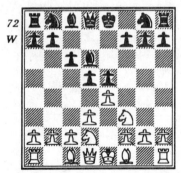

By adopting a more classical approach, Black not only saves a tempo by leaving out ... g6, but also keeps watch over the queenside (this is sometimes difficult with the bishop on g7 being blocked in by the e5-pawn).

5 g3

5 ♕e2 is worth consideration, and does have the merit of bypassing Black's possibility mentioned in the next note, because of the indirect threat to the e-pawn. Ljubojevic – Bouaziz, Szirak Interzonal 1987, continued 5 ... ♕e7 6 g3 ♘f6 7 ♗g2 0–0 8 0–0 dxe4 9 dxe4 ♘bd7 10 ♘c4 with a minuscule edge to White.

5 ... ♘f6

An ambitious continuation is 5 ... ♘e7, intending a quick strike with ... f5. Not surprisingly, this may prove to be a somewhat hopeful plan, and after 6 ♗g2 0–0 7 0–0 f5 White should follow fundamental principles and react immediately by hitting back in the centre with 8 c4!, e.g. 8 ... dxe4 9 dxe4

♘a6 10 a3 f4 11 b4 when White's initiative on the queenside and pressure against the black e-pawn outweigh Black's progress on the kingside.

In the game Schuyler – Song, Chicago 1989, Black gave the game another character by pushing his f-pawn only one square, but White obtained a better game: 7 ... f6 8 a3 ♗e6 9 ♖e1 ♕d7 10 d4! ♗g4 11 c4! exd4 12 cxd5 c5 13 ♕b3 ♘g6 14 ♘c4 and White eventually broke through with e4 – e5.

6 ♗g2 0–0
7 0–0 ♖e8

The most popular home for the rook. Black experimented with 7 ... ♕c7!? in Howell – Wells, Swansea 1987, preferring to use the d-file for the rook. There followed 8 ♖e1 ♗e6 9 c3?! (this makes d3 a target and invites ... ♖d8; 9 h3 is preferable, when 9 ... ♖d8 10 ♕e2 ♘bd7 allows 11 ♘g5) 9 ... ♖d8 10 ♕e2 ♘bd7 11 h3 h6 12 ♘h4 ♗f8 13 ♕f3 ♘c5 14 ♘f5 ♗xf5 15 exf5 e4! and White found himself on the defensive. In fact mass exchanges did not loosen Black's grip on the game: 16 dxe4 dxe4 17 ♕e2 ♘d3 18 ♖f1 e3! 19 ♕xe3 ♗c5 20 ♕e2 (not 20 ♕f3 ♘xc1 21 ♖axc1 ♖xd2) 20 ... ♕xg3 21 ♕f3 ♕xf3 22 ♘xf3 ♘e4 23 ♘d4 ♗xd4 24 ♗xe4 ♗b6 25 ♔g2 ♘xc1 26 ♖axc1 ♖d2 27 ♖c2 ♖ad8 28 ♖fc1 ♗xf2 29 ♖xd2 ♖xd2 30 ♖c2 ♗e3+ and Black went on to win.

8 h3

Once again Black will have difficulties developing his queen's bishop.

8 ... a5

A sensible move, as Black seems to do best looking to the queenside for play. Concentrating on the kingside with 8 ... ♘bd7 9 ♖e1 ♘f8 is also possible, although the plan of b3 and ♗b2 still leaves White slightly better.

9 ♖e1 dxe4

Without doubt the safest choice at Black's disposal, aiming for equality by producing a symmetrical pawn structure. This is undoubtedly an improvement on 9 ... ♘a6, as in Sax – Martin, Hastings 1983/84, which saw White seize a safe advantage with 10 d4! dxe4 11 ♘xe5.

10 dxe4 ♗c5
11 c3?!

An inaccuracy which Black immediately profits from. Better is 11 a4, preventing the following cramping advance.

11 ... a4! (73)

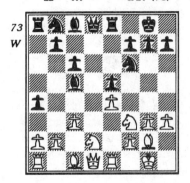

Severely limiting White's queenside options. Consequently Anand prepares a manoeuvre which will transfer his queen's knight from d2 to f5. Although this is a thematic and, indeed, good idea, it would be all the more potent if Black did not enjoy a considerable territorial stake on the queenside.

12 ♕c2

Not the immediate 12 ♘f1? ♕xd1 13 ♖xd1 ♘xe4.

12 ... ♘bd7
13 ♘f1 h6
14 ♘e3 ♗f8
15 ♘f5 ♘c5

Black has countered the knight sortie by finding a similarly useful outpost.

16 ♖d1 ♕c7
17 ♘h2!? (74)

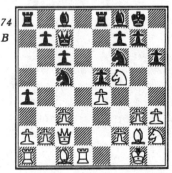

This move is not at all rare in several variations of this opening. White adds support to the e-pawn and threatens to put the knight on g4, whence further pressure will be added to f6 and h6 (and the e-pawn). If Black exchanges on g4 White then has an extra g-pawn (after hxg4) with which to throw at the enemy king's pawn cover.

17 ...   ♘e6
18 ♗e3   ♖ed8!

Black takes over the d-file thanks to the fact that White is tied to the defence of his weak a2-pawn (19 a3 ♘b3!).

19 ♖xd8   ♖xd8
20 ♘g4

Removing the irritating a-pawn is too dangerous: 20 ♗xc5 ♘xc5 21 ♕xa4 ♖d2 hits both f2 and b2.

20 ...   ♘xg4
21 hxg4   b5

White's kingside attack lacks punch, so Black continues to improve his queenside. All this was made possible because of White's slip on move 11.

22 g5   hxg5
23 ♗xg5   f6
24 ♗e3   ♕d7!

White must keep the queens on the board or stand worse in an ending, so this clever move undermines Anand's defence of the e-pawn by threatening ... ♕d3.

25 ♗f1   ♕f7
26 c4

Better than the positionally suicidal 26 a3 ♘b3. This way White should eventually win back his pawn, leaving the c6- and a4-pawns as potential targets.

26 ...   bxc4
27 ♗xc5   ♗xc5

28 a3   ♔h7

Black vacates the a2 - g8 diagonal in anticipation of White capturing on c4.

29 ♖c1   ♕g6

Since it takes time for White to recoup his slight material loss, Black shifts his attentions to creating his opponent problems on the other flank.

30 ♔g2

Black threatened 30 ... ♘xf5 followed by 31 ... ♕xg3+, so White promptly unpins his f2-pawn.

30 ...   ♕g5
31 ♗xc4   ♖d2 *(75)*

75
W

Ostensibly the killing blow, but Anand manages to stay in the game by giving up his queen for a rook and bishop.

32 ♗xe6!   ♖xc2
33 ♖xc2   ♘d4
34 ♖xc6   ♕d2

This time the black queen invades and threatens the f-pawn. Preventing this with 35 ♘xd4 gives Black a dangerous passed pawn after 35 ... exd4, so how does White survive?

35 ♖c7!

White's rook, bishop and knight work just as harmoniously as the black queen and bishop. Anand's threat is 36 ♖xg7+ ♔h8 37 ♖g8+ ♔h7 38 ♖g7+. Malaniuk gets in a few checks of his own, but there is nothing more.

35	...	♕xf2+
36	♔h3	♕f1+
37	♔g4	♕d1+
38	♔h3	♕h1+
39	♔g4	♕xe4+
40	♔h3	♕h1+
41	♔g4	♕d1+
42	♔h4	♕h1+
43	♔g4	♕e4+
44	♔h3	♕h1+

½–½

5 Black Plays ... ♗g4

This system arises most commonly after the following sequence of moves:

1	♘f3	d5
2	g3	c6
3	♗g2	♗g4 (76)

76
W

The ... ♗g4 variation is very popular with players of all levels. So often a piece with which Black has problems, the queen's bishop immediately finds a home, allowing Black the option of establishing a solid pawn centre with ... e6 without closing the bishop out of play.

When Black erects the c6 - d5 - e6 pawn wall, the king's knight usually comes to f6 and the bishop to e7, and after furthering his development Black might attempt to push forward with ... e6 - e5. Using the same pawn structure, Black can also play ... ♗d6 and ... ♘e7, when the idea is that the freedom of the f-pawn should compensate for no longer attacking the e4-square.

White almost always hits the queen's bishop with h2 - h3, giving Black the choice of whether or not to surrender the bishop pair. Generally, this is only a good idea if the resulting simplification decreases White's attacking potential. It is better to preserve the tension and retreat to h5. Having said this, it is surprising how many masters make the mistake of voluntarily exchanging on f3. In general, White's space advantage and attacking possibilities give him a good game, and Black's position also lacks flexibility.

A more aggressive course of action for Black is the early advance ... e7 - e5, staking a claim for a share of the space in the centre. White is then able to put pressure on the e-pawn, and the f5-square is available for the king's knight.

This sometimes leads to Black simplifying by ... dxe4 or relieving the pressure on e5 by taking on f3, both of which are to White's advantage.

Another important feature of the ... ♗g4 variation is Black's pin on the d1 – h5 diagonal. Because the King's Indian Attack centres around White pushing with e2 – e4, a dual-purpose move here is ♕e1. This is a good square, as not only does White escape the pin, releasing the king's knight to pressure e5 and, in the case of ... e5 from Black, threatening ♘f3 – h4 – f5, but also the queen helps support the advance of the e-pawn.

White Plays an Early e4

Biyiasas – Vasyukov
Hastings 1978/79

1	♘f3	♘f6
2	g3	d5
3	♗g2	c6
4	0-0	♗g4
5	d3	e6
6	♘bd2	♘bd7
7	e4	(77)

White can also put the question to the bishop here with 7 h3. This should transpose to the game, but a surprising number of players exchange on f3. Vasyukov – Trifunovic, USSR vs Yugoslavia 1963, continued 7 h3 ♗xf3?! 8 ♘xf3 ♗c5 9 ♕e1 0-0 10 e4 dxe4

11 dxe4 e5 12 ♗g5 h6 13 ♗d2 ♖e8 14 ♖d1 ♕c7 15 ♘h4! with a good game for White.

In the game Kogan – Seirawan, USA 1985, the American Grandmaster voluntarily gave White the bishop pair after 1 ♘f3 d5 2 g3 c6 3 ♗g2 ♗g4 4 0-0 e6 5 d3 ♗xf3?!. The idea here is that the recapture ♘xf3 is not possible, but after 6 ♗xf3 ♘f6 7 ♘d2 ♘bd7 8 e4 ♗c5 9 ♕e2 dxe4, 10 ♘xe4! (instead of 10 dxe4) would have given White the advantage.

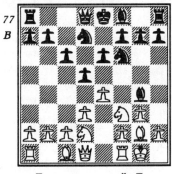

77
B

7	...	♗e7
8	♖e1	

An alternative is 8 ♕e1. Then, after the moves 8 ... 0-0 9 h3 ♗h5 we reach an important position. Continuing as in our main game with 10 e5 leaves White a little awkwardly placed after 10 ... ♘e8 11 ♘h2 ♕b6!, so Gutman – Farago, Brussels 1986, went 10 ♔h1!? ♘e8 11 ♘g1! ♘c7 12 ♘b3 dxe4 13 dxe4 e5 14 ♕a5! ♘e6 15 f4! with a slight advantage to White.

The game Karasev – Klovan, Podolsk 1990, saw some interesting manoeuvring. Instead of 10 e5, White played 10 ♘h2 e5 11 ♘df3 dxe4 12 dxe4 ♘e8 13 ♕c3! (an excellent move which – like Gutman's 14 ♕a5! – highlights the usefulness of placing the queen on e1; now 13 ... f6 is met by 14 ♕b3+ and 15 ♕xb7, while 13 ... ♕c7 prevents the desired plan of ... ♘e8 – c7 – e6) 13 ... ♘d6 14 ♕e3 ♕b6 15 ♕e2 with the better game, thanks to Black's knight on d6. The rest of the game is entertaining: 15 ... ♖fd8 16 ♘g4 f6 17 b3 ♗f7 18 ♘h4 ♗f8 19 ♖d1 ♘b5 20 ♖xd7! ♖xd7 21 ♘xf6+ gxf6 22 ♕g4+ ♗g7 23 ♕xd7 ♖d8 24 ♕e7 ♖d1+ 25 ♔h2 ♘d4 (in return for the pawn Black has a bind, but White has seen further; note that 25 ... ♕xf2 26 ♗e3! ♕e2 27 ♖xd1 ♕xd1 28 ♕xb7 helps White) 26 ♗a3!! ♖xa1 27 ♗c5! ♕xc5 (forced, e.g. 27 ... ♕a5 28 b4 ♕xa2 29 ♕d8+ ♗f8 30 ♕xf8 mate) 28 ♕xc5 ♖xa2 29 ♘f5 ♖xc2 30 ♘e7+ ♔f8 31 ♕d6 ♔e8 32 ♘c8 ♗f8 33 ♕xf6 c5 34 ♕xe5+ ♔d7 35 ♕b8 1-0.

8	...	0-0
9	h3	♗h5
10	e5	♘e8 (78)

This is the type of position White was aiming for with 8 ♖e1. Unlike French Defence-related positions Black has his queen's bishop outside his pawns, but the cost of this luxury is a delay in beginning the thematic queenside attack. White, meanwhile, is able to play in the classic King's Indian Attack style...

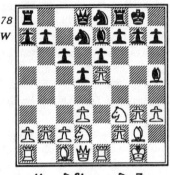

78
W

| 11 | ♘f1 | ♘c7 |

A similar position arose in the game Todorcevic - Lukacs, Rome 1988. After 1 ♘f3 d5 2 g3 ♘f6 3 ♗g2 c6 4 d3 ♗g4 5 ♘bd2 (a clever move order which guarantees to keep a knight on f3 should Black decide to give up the two bishops) 5 ... e6 6 0-0 ♗e7 7 h3 ♗h5 8 e4 0-0 9 ♕e2!? ♘bd7 10 ♖e1 a5 11 e5 ♘e8 12 ♘f1 ♘c7, White played 13 g4! ♗g6 14 ♘g3 h6 15 ♗f4 b5 16 ♕d2! c5 17 g5! with considerable pressure on the kingside.

12	♘1h2	a5
13	♗f4	a4
14	♕d2	

Also to be considered is 14 a3 to prevent any weakening of the dark squares.

| 14 | ... | a3 |
| 15 | b3 | ♘b5?! |

Black has little time for such a provocative move. Better is 15 ... c5 followed by ... b5 – b4 and only then ... ♘b5.

| 16 | c4! | ♘c7 |
| 17 | h4 | ♗xf3 |

White threatened to win by
18 g4 and 19 h5, but preserving
the bishop with 17 ... Qg6 may
have been a lesser evil.

18	Nxf3	Na6
19	Red1	Bb4
20	Wc2	Wa5
21	Rac1	d4!? (79)

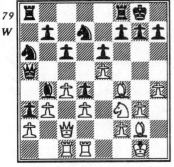

Consistent with Black's plan
of dark-square pressure. Now,
instead of 22 Nxd4? allowing
22 ... Nxe5, White prepares to
infiltrate on the kingside and
subsequently force either ... g6
or ... h6.

22	We2	Bc3
23	Ng5	g6
24	h5	

A typical pawn-thrust in this
opening, serving to open the
h-file when the time is right.

24	...	Nac5
25	Wg4	Rfe8
26	Wh4	Nf8
27	Ne4!	

With this move White shows
that, despite exchanging his
dominant knight for its passive
counterpart, the attack will
proceed unhindered. Indeed,
Black can only try to regroup

and wait for the invasion.

27	...	Nxe4
28	Bxe4	Qb4
29	Kg2!	

Clearing the way for the
white rooks to join in the
attack.

29	...	Wd8
30	Wg4	Ra5
31	hxg6	fxg6

An even more immediate end
would result from 31 ... hxg6 as
White could simply double on
the h-file. The move played
puts up more resistance, but
Black's position is by now far
from invulnerable.

32	Rh1	Wd7
33	Rh6	Re7
34	Rch1	Rg7
35	Bg5! (80)	

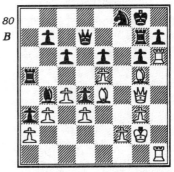

35	...	Rxe5

The best try, as 35 ... Qe7
fails to 36 Bf6 Bxf6 37 exf6 Rf7
when White breaks through
with 38 Bxg6! Nxg6 39 Wxg6+!.

36	Bf6	Ra5
37	Bxg7	Wxg7
38	Rxh7!	

Forcing decisive material
gain.

| 38 | ... | ♘xh7 |
| 39 | ♕xe6+ | ♔f8 |

The ending which would result after 39 ... ♕f7 40 ♕xf7+ ♔xf7 41 ♖xh7+ ♔f6 42 ♖xb7 is hopeless for Black (e.g. 42 ... c5 43 ♖b6+).

| 40 | ♗xg6 | ♕e7 |

Or 40 ... ♘f6 41 ♖h8+!

| 41 | ♕c8+ | 1-0 |

Black's queenside play came to naught.

Korchnoi – Flear
Lugano 1986

1	♘f3	d5
2	g3	♘f6
3	♗g2	c6
4	0-0	♗g4
5	d3	e6
6	♕e1!?	(81)

There is nothing wrong in playing this standard move so early.

6	...	♘bd7
7	e4	dxe4
8	dxe4	e5
9	♘bd2	♗c5
10	♘c4	

Korchnoi takes advantage of the extra move caused by Black's ... e6 followed by ... e5. Now, thanks to 6 ♕e1, White threatens 11 ♘fxe5.

| 10 | ... | ♕e7 |
| 11 | ♘e3 | h5!? |

The English Grandmaster tries to revitalise his game by introducing a theoretical novelty. 11 ... ♗e6 12 ♘f5 is clearly bad for Black, so giving up the bishop pair with 11...♗xe3 12 ♕xe3 is the lesser evil, with an advantage to White. The game now takes on an unusual character for this variation, and the reader would be well advised to see how former World Championship challenger Viktor Korchnoi shows us the King's Indian Attack is indeed aptly named – wherever Black's king hides!

| 12 | a3! | 0-0-0 | (82) |

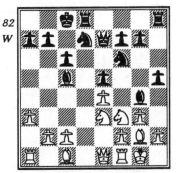

| 13 | b4 | ♗d6 |

Better than 13 ... ♗b6 14 a4 and 15 a5.

| 14 | ♘h4! | g6 |

Black would like to attack with 14 ... g5, but this gives away the f5-square.

| 15 | c4 | ♘h7 |

Intending ... ♘g5 to eye the weak h3-square.

16	h3	♗e6
17	♕c3!	♔b8
18	♖d1	♗c7
19	♗b2	♘g5
20	♔h2	♘f6
21	♕c2	♗c8

A dual-purpose move which both bolsters the king's position and makes way for the attacking manoeuvre ... ♘g5 - e6 - d4. Another possibility is 21 ... ♖xd1 22 ♖xd1 ♖d8 23 ♖xd8+ ♕xd8, but 24 c5 grants White more space and a slight advantage on both sides of the board.

Korchnoi now goes on the offensive:

| 22 | b5!? | ♘e6 |
| 23 | bxc6 | ♘d4?! |

Faced with the dismal prospect of 23 ... bxc6 24 ♖ab1 ♗b7, Black decides to complicate matters.

| 24 | ♗xd4 | exd4 |
| 25 | cxb7 | ♗xh3! *(83)* |

Not 25 ... dxe3? 26 bxc8=♕+ ♔xc8 27 f4 with a terrible

position for Black.

| 26 | ♘d5! | ♘xd5 |
| 27 | cxd5 | ♗g4! |

Again not 27 ... ♕xh4? 28 ♕xc7+!.

| 28 | ♔g1! |

Unfortunately for Black, his energetic counter-attacking forces a nice exchange sacrifice from Korchnoi.

| 28 | ... | ♗xd1 |

Consistent and tempting, but 28 ... g5!? 29 ♘f3 ♗xf3 30 ♗xf3 g4 31 ♗g2 h4 may have given White more problems.

| 29 | ♖xd1 | ♕xa3 |
| 30 | ♘f3! |

Threatening ♘xd4 - c6.

30	...	♕c3
31	♕b1	♗b6
32	♘e5!	♖d6

In answer to the push 32 ... d3 White has 33 ♘c6+ ♔xb7 34 ♖xd3 ♕c5 35 ♕b2!, maintaining the decisive attack by simultaneously defending f2 and threatening ♖c3.

33	♖c1!	♕a3
34	♘c4	♕c5
35	e5!	♖dd8

Or 35 ... ♖xd5 36 ♘xb6!, e.g. 36 ... ♕xb6 37 ♕xb6 axb6 38 ♗xd5.

| 36 | ♘d6! | ♕a3 |
| 37 | ♕c2! | 1-0 |

Black cannot safely escape the threat of 38 ♕c8+!. If 37 ... a6 38 ♕c8+ ♖xc8 39 ♖xc8+ ♖xc8 (39 ... ♔a7 40 b8=♕ mate) 40 bxc8=♕+ ♔a7 41 ♕b7 mate.

A fine attacking game by Viktor Korchnoi.

White Fianchettoes Queenside

Spiridonov – Shamkovich
Tbilisi 1970

1	♘f3	d5
2	g3	c6
3	d3	

Once again, in anticipation of the ... ♗g4 variation, White chooses to support his knight on f3 with 3 d3 and 4 ♘bd2 before playing ♗g2.

3	...	♗g4
4	♘bd2	♘f6
5	♗g2	e6
6	h3	♗h5

Exchanging with 6 ... ♗xf3 is even less advisable now, thanks to White's move order.

7	0-0	♗e7

Black can also play ... ♗d6 with the aim of a future push with ... e6 – e5. This plan will be examined later.

8	b3 *(84)*

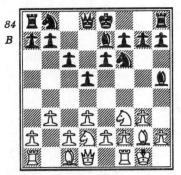

84
B

Treating the variation in this manner, with two fianchettoed bishops, is a very attractive plan. White completes his development and pressurises Black down the long a1 – h8 diagonal. His pieces are well coordinated and are ready for action in any sector of the board.

8	...	0-0
9	♗b2	♘bd7

Hübner – I. Farago, Wijk aan Zee 1988, went 9 ... a5 10 a4 ♘bd7 11 e3!?. After 11 ... h6 12 ♕e2 ♘c5 13 g4 ♗g6 14 ♘e5 ♗h7 15 f4 White had an excellent position. The idea of holding back the e-pawn is interesting.

10	e4	a5

A logical continuation which Black often employs in systems based on ... ♗g4 or ... ♗f5. It is a matter of taste whether White answers ... a5 with a4 or a3, although the former is generally more popular. Black will endeavour to open up the queenside with the plan of ... b5 and ... bxa4, meeting ♖xa4 with ... ♘b6/c5 followed by ... a4, or bxa4 with play on the b-file and against White's a-pawn. Circumstances will dictate White's choice of approach. In this particular game, White has calculated precisely that the placing of his opponent's pieces could embarrass Black should the latter persevere with the standard queenside attack against 11 a3.

11	a3	♕b6

In Spiridonov – Hennings, Orebro 1966, Black developed with 11... ♘c5 12 ♕e2 ♕c7. After 13 g4! ♗g6 14 ♘e5 dxe4 15 dxe4

♘fd7 16 f4! f6 17 ♘xg6 hxg6 18 e5 White stood much better.

12 ♕e2   a4?

Although this is the usual method of battering White's queenside, it falls into Spiridonov's trap. A better – albeit slower – continuation would be 12 ... ♕a6! with the idea of 13 c4 dxc4!? followed by 14 ... ♖fd8.

13 b4

It would be wrong to allow ... axb3, leaving White with a weak a-pawn. Black's pawn structure, on the other hand, would be very solid, and this fact, combined with pressure on the a-file, would give Black the advantage.

13 ...   c5?

All according to plan, but it is White who has the more stable position.

14 exd5   exd5?!

Instead 14 ... ♘xd5 is met by the natural 15 ♘c4 with a White advantage, since Black's aggression has resulted in producing weaknesses in his own camp. However, in recapturing with the pawn Shamkovich has grossly underestimated the potential power of White's minor pieces.

15 ♕xe7!   ♖fe8

Winning the queen, but at what cost?

16 ♗xf6!   ♖xe7

Not 16 ... ♘xf6?? 17 ♕xc5.

17 ♗xe7 (85)

In return for his queen White has a rook, bishop and

knight. The next step is to use his domination of the dark squares to create unchallengeable outposts for his strongest pieces.

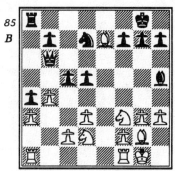

| 17 | ... | ♕c7 |
| 18 | ♖fe1 | f6 |

A dual-purpose move which both adds to Black's limited claim to the dark squares and prepares to defend the d-pawn with ... ♗f7.

19	bxc5	♘xc5
20	♘d4	♗f7
21	♘b5!	♕d7
22	♗xc5	♕xb5
23	♗b4!	

A wonderful square for the bishop. Black's problem is that there is precious little for his queen to attack, while White's harmonious pieces, aided by his control of the dark squares, remain flexible.

| 23 | ... | ♖e8 |
| 24 | c4! | |

White uses his other bishop to challenge the enemy pawns.

24	...	♕d7
25	♖xe8+	♕xe8
26	cxd5	♕e5

27 ♖d1!

A simple but effective plan. After the forced exchange of his bishop Black will have the hopeless task of blockading the d-pawn with his lone queen, so White prepares for the push.

27	...	♗xd5
28	♘c4	♕d4
29	♗xd5+	♕xd5 *(86)*

30	♘e3	♕d4
31	♘c2	♕b2
32	♖d2	♕b1+
33	♔h2	1-0

An interesting game which shows how well White's pieces work together in this opening. Despite playing normal, even thematic, moves on the queen-side, Black suddenly found himself in a terrible position. White's move order in the above game was designed to answer an eventual ... ♗xf3 with ♘xf3, rather than have to recapture with the bishop. Readers who may want to couple this idea with the plan of fianchettoing the queen's bishop should avoid the following trap: Ribli - Geller, Buda-pest 1973, saw an important idea after the opening moves 1 ♘f3 ♘f6 2 g3 d5 3 ♗g2 c6 4 b3 ♗g4 5 ♗b2 ♘bd7 6 d3 e6 7 ♘bd2 ♗e7. White automatically 'hit' the bishop with 8 h3?!. Black played 8 ... ♗xf3!? when White's only way to play for an advantage is 9 ♗xf3, as after 9 ♘xf3?! Black can take advantage of White's uncastled king with 9 ... ♗a3! 10 ♗xa3 ♕a5+ with equality.

Jansa - Keene
Aarhus 1983

1	g3	♘f6
2	♘f3	d5
3	♗g2	c6
4	0-0	♗g4
5	b3	

Here Jansa makes use of a move order designed to prevent an early ... e5 from Black.

5	...	♘bd7
6	♗b2	e6
7	d3	♗d6
8	♘bd2	0-0
9	♕e1	

The immediate 9 e4 is also possible, when 9 ... dxe4 10 dxe4 ♗e5!? is interesting, taking advantage of the pin.

9	...	e5

Losing a tempo compared with lines in which the Black e-pawn reaches this square in one move. Black's compensation lies in his being able to properly organise his position before the push.

10	e4	♖e8
11	h3	♗h5
12	♘h4!	*(87)*

With his development completed White undertakes action on the kingside. The diagram position has arisen – by different routes – often in international chess. White has a choice of plans.

In Spraggett – Chernin, Paris 1989, Black played 12 ... ♘f8, hoping to meet the aggressive 13 f4 with 13 ... dxe4 14 dxe4 exf4 15 gxf4 ♘g6!. White, however, elected to fight for light-square control by opening up the centre with 13 exd5!? ♘xd5 (White's King's Indian Attack bishop would have command of the long h1 – a8 diagonal after 13 ... exd5 14 c4!) 14 ♘df3! ♕d7 15 c4!? ♘b4 16 ♕e4. White has more control and stands better. The game continued 16... ♗c7 17 ♖ad1! ♖ad8 (not 17 ... ♘xa2 18 d4! exd4 19 ♕b1! ♘b4 20 ♖xd4 when, for the sacrificed pawn, White has a horde of pieces ready to attack the opposing

king) 18 a3! ♘c2 (White's d-pawn is also 'poisoned', as after 18 ... ♘xd3 19 b4 traps the knight), and now 19 ♖d2! ♘d4 20 ♘xd4 exd4 21 ♕f5 was necessary, preserving White's advantage.

| 12 | ... | ♘c5 |

Now Spraggett's interesting idea is out of the question as 13 exd5 cxd5 14 c4 loses to 14 ... ♘xd3.

| 13 | ♘f5 | ♗c7 |
| 14 | f4! | |

White voluntarily places his centre under fire so as to open up lines against Black's king.

14	...	exf4
15	gxf4	dxe4
16	♘xe4!	

In answer to 16 dxe4 Black can turn the tables with 16 ... ♗a5! 17 ♕g3 ♗g6.

| 16 | ... | ♘fxe4 |
| 17 | dxe4 | |

Jansa gives 17 ♘xg7!? as an adventurous alternative. Black's best is 17 ... ♘f6, when 18 ♘xe8? is a mistake on account of 18 ... ♘xe8 19 ♕c3 f6 (20 ♕xc5?? ♗b6). Instead 18 ♗xf6! ♖xe1 19 ♗xd8 ♖xa1 20 ♖xa1 ♖xd8 21 ♘xh5 results in a position in which Black has some compensation for the pawn deficit.

The game move is not so hazardous, and guarantees a powerful initiative even after Black's most accurate defence.

| 17 | ... | ♘e6! |

The only move. Attempting

to cut off White's queen's bishop with 17 ... f6? does not work, e.g. 18 ♕h4 ♗g6 19 ♖ad1 ♕c8 20 ♘xg7!.

18 ♕g3   ♗g6

18 ... f6 still helps White – 19 ♕h4 ♗g6 20 ♖ad1 ♕b8 (Or 20 ... ♕c8 21 ♘d6) 21 ♖d7! ♗xf5 22 exf5 ♘xf4 23 ♖xg7+! is one possible way for Black to lose.

19 ♖ad1 *(88)*

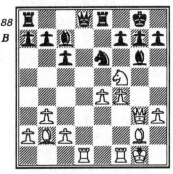

19 ...   ♘xf4!?

Jansa criticises this try, offering instead 19 ... ♕b8 ('!' Jansa) 20 ♘xg7 ♘xg7 21 ♕c3 f6! 22 ♕xf6 ♘h5 23 ♕h8+ ♔f7 24 ♕c3 as Black's best resource. However, White has two pawns and a dangerous attack for his sacrificed piece, so Black's move must be considered the lesser evil.

20 ♕xf4!   ♗xf4

Not 20 ... ♕xd1? 21 ♕xc7 ♕xc2 22 ♗xg7 ♗xf5 23 ♖xf5 with a won game for White.

21	**♖xd8**	**♖axd8**
22	**♖xf4**	**♖d1+**
23	**♖f1**	**♖ed8**
24	**♗c3**	

Preventing a future ... ♖d2.

24 ... f6 25 ♔f2 ♗xf5 26 exf5 and White's bishops are stronger than a rook.

The plan of developing the king's bishop on d6 and the knight on e7 is designed to keep out of harm's way, enabling Black to attack on the queenside:

**Lazic – Dizdar
Yugoslav Ch 1990**

1	♘f3	d5
2	g3	♗g4
3	♗g2	c6
4	0-0	♘d7
5	d3	e6
6	♘bd2	♗d6
7	♕e1	

White does not have to move his queen away from the d1 – h5 diagonal, although he must subsequently be prepared to meet ... ♘e5 at some point, when Black intends to exchange a couple of minor pieces. The game Damljanovic – Kosic, Yugoslav Ch 1990, proceeded in this manner. White played 7 e4 ♘e7 8 h3 ♗h5 9 ♘b3!?. After 9 ... ♘e5 10 ♕e2 ♗xf3 11 ♗xf3 ♘xf3+ 12 ♕xf3 0-0 13 ♔g2 dxe4 14 dxe4 e5 15 ♖d1 ♕c7 16 ♗e3 ♖ad8 17 ♕e2 ♘c8 18 a4 ♗e7 19 a5 White had a slight edge.

7 ...   ♘e7 *(89)*

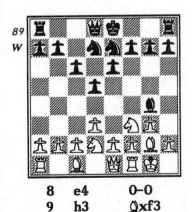

8	e4	0-0
9	h3	♗xf3

9 ... ♗h5 transposes to Lazic
- Dzevlan, Yugoslav Ch 1991.
White immediately began operations on the kingside with 10
♘h4 ♕b8 11 f4, when Black
countered with the thematic 11
... f5. The game continued 12
exd5 exd5 13 ♘df3 ♖e8 14 ♕f2
♗c5 15 ♗e3 ♗xe3+ 16 ♕xe3 ♘g6
17 ♕d4 ♗xf3 (better is 17 ...
♘xh4 18 ♘xh4 with White
having a positional advantage)
18 ♘xf5! ♘f6 19 ♗xf3, and
White eventually converted his
extra pawn into a win.

10	♘xf3	♕b6
11	♔h1	a5
12	♘d2	a4
13	♖b1	a3

Of course, White could have
played 13 a3 to prevent the
following weakening of the
dark squares on the queenside,
but Lazic judges that the advanced a-pawn may prove to be
more of a liability than an asset
if Black overplays his hand.

14	b3	♗b4
15	♕e2	♗c3

16 b4!

An excellent move which
aims to prevent Black from
taking control of the queenside.

| | 16 | ... | ♖a4 |

Not 16 ... ♗xb4? 17 c3.

17	♖b3!	♗b2
18	♗xb2	axb2
19	a3	♘c8
20	♘b1!	(90)

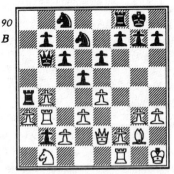

White is about to safely take
the b2-pawn, leaving Black
with no compensation.

Black Plays an Early ... e5

To end this chapter we shall
look at two games in which
Black plays an early ... e5.

Damljanovic – C. Hansen
New York Open 1987

1	g3	d5
2	♘f3	♘f6
3	♗g2	c6
4	0-0	♗g4
5	d3	♘bd7
6	♘bd2	

Grandmaster Lev Gutman is
fond of the immediate 6 ♕e1.

The game Gutman – Smejkal, West Germany 1987, saw White maintain the usual slight advantage after 6 ... e5 7 e4 dxe4 (better than 7 ... d4?! 8 c3! c5 9 ♘a3) 8 dxe4 ♗e7 9 ♘bd2 0-0 10 h3! ♗h5 11 ♘c4 ♕c7 12 a4 ♖fe8 13 ♗d2 ♗f8 14 ♗c3 ♗xf3 15 ♗xf3 b5 16 axb5.

Two years later in Gutman – Rogers, Moscow Open 1989, Black deviated from 8 ... ♗e7 with the premature 8 ... ♗xf3. There followed 9 ♗xf3 ♗c5 10 ♘d2 0-0 11 ♘c4 ♕e7 12 ♗d2 ♘b6 13 ♘e3 ♕e6 14 b3 g6 15 a4 ♖ad8 16 ♕e2 ♖fe8 17 ♖ad1 h5 18 ♗g2 ♔g7 19 a5! ♘a8 20 ♕c4! ♕e7, when 21 c3! (followed by b3 – b4) would have left White considerably better. Instead, Gutman played the faulty 21 b4?, allowing 21 ... ♖xd2! 22 ♖xd2 ♗xb4 23 ♖d3 ♗xa5.

6   ...   e5 *(91)*

One advantage of an early ... e5 is that Black no longer has to worry about a future e4 – e5 from White. Also, a tempo is saved compared with those lines in which Black first plays

... e6 and then ... e5. However, the early advance may result in the e5-pawn being a weakness, and Black has less control over the squares d5 and f5.

7   h3   ♗h5
8   e4   dxe4

In Kir. Georgiev – Torre, Saint John 1988, Black retained the central tension with 8 ... ♗d6. The game continued 9 ♕e1 0-0 10 ♘h4 ♖e8 11 f4 exf4 12 gxf4 dxe4 13 dxe4 ♘d5 with a menacing position for Black. White had calculated well, though, for after 14 ♘c4 ♗c5+ 15 ♔h1 ♘7b6 16 ♘e5 ♘b4 17 ♘f5 ♗g6 (17 ... ♘xc2 18 ♕c3) 18 ♕c3 ♗f8 19 ♘g3 ♕c7 20 ♗e3 the roles had changed and Black was defending.

9   dxe4   ♗c5
10 ♕e1   ♗xf3

In the game Kindermann – Gelfand, Munich 1991, Black did not worry about a possible ♘f3 – h4 from White, preferring to keep his bishop pair for a little longer: 10 ... 0-0 11 ♘c4 ♖e8 12 a4 ♕c7 13 ♘h4! ♗f8 14 ♗g5! with a more active position for White. The 'automatic' 14 ... h6?! is simply met by 15 ♗d2 ♘c5 16 g4 ♗g6 17 ♘xg6 fxg6 18 f4, while 14 ... b5 weakens the d5-square after 15 axb5 cxb5 16 ♘e3. Best for Black is 14 ... ♗g6 15 ♖d1 h6 16 ♗xf6 ♘xf6 17 ♘xg6 fxg6 18 h4, when White has a minuscule edge.

11 ♗xf3

The recapture with the

bishop is better here as White wants to deploy his remaining knight on c4, whence it will pressure the squares a5, b6, d6 and e5.

| 11 | ... | 0-0 |
| 12 | a4 | |

An important and common move, fighting for space on the queenside and aiming to secure an outpost on c4 for the knight. Now a future ... b5 from Black gives White the a-file after axb5 and, assuming Black in turn takes back with the c-pawn, further weakens the d5-square.

12	...	♕e7
13	♕e2	a5
14	♘c4	♘e8

Beginning one of Black's more desirable manoeuvres (... ♘f6 - e8 - c7 - e6), but at the cost of structural weaknesses on the queenside. The alternative, 14 ... ♘b6, would force White to switch his attentions to the kingside after 15 ♘e3 g6 16 h4, with the usual slight advantage.

| 15 | ♗d2 | b6 |
| 16 | ♗g4! | (92) |

Redeploying the bishop on another diagonal.

16	...	♘c7
17	♔g2	♘e6
18	c3	g6
19	♗h6	♖fe8
20	h4	f6
21	♖ad1	♘df8
22	h5!	

Keep an eye on White's

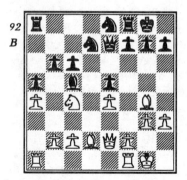

h-pawn.

22	...	♖ad8
23	♘c1	♖xd1
24	♖xd1	♖d8
25	♖h1!	

It is often very useful for White in these positions to exchange one pair of rooks and keep the other on the board. In this way White can attack on the kingside without the possibility of a dangerous counter from Black down the d-file. Here Black's coming invasion is aimed at relieving the pressure rather than producing threats.

| 25 | ... | ♕d7 |
| 26 | ♕f3 | ♕d3 |

A forced concession. Black must enter into a disadvantageous endgame rather than sit back and let White dictate matters. If 26 ... ♕e7 27 ♗e3! eyes Black's weak b-pawn whilst at the same time keeping a threatening stance on the kingside. Even worse for Black is 26 ... ♕f7?, e.g. 27 hxg6 hxg6 28 ♘xe5! fxe5 29 ♖h8+! ♔g7 30 ♗h6+.

| 27 | ♕xd3 | ♖xd3 |

White has a much better game. Now 28 ♗d1 is a good move, intending to take up residence on the a2 - g8 diagonal, but White brings his king to the centre instead.

28	♔f1	♖d8
29	♔e2	♔f7
30	f3?!	

Another slight inaccuracy, although White is still well on top. Better was 30 f4 or 30 ♗e3.

30	...	♘g7
31	h6	♘e8!
32	♗e3!	♗xe3
33	♔xe3	♘d6!

A clever way of distracting White's attention from Black's weak queenside. If now 34 ♘xb6? ♖b8 is good for Black. Instead White creates a passed pawn in order to maintain his initiative.

34	♘xd6+	♖xd6
35	b4	axb4

Otherwise White will invade down the b-file, e.g. 35 ... ♖d8 36 bxa5 bxa5 37 ♖b1 when Black's a- and c-pawns would make easy targets for White.

36	cxb4	♖d4
37	♖b1	♔e7
38	a5!	b5

Leaving White with a b-pawn to worry about.

| 39 | f4 | |

White waits to reach the time control. The more direct 39 a6 was better.

39	...	♘d7
40	♖b3	♘b8

41	♗c8!	

Threatening 42 a6.

41	...	♔d8
42	♗e6!	♘a6
43	♗g8!	(93)

White's middlegame pressure on the kingside - particularly the advance h4 - h5 - h6 - also served another purpose, as Black will now have to contend with another outside passed pawn. Note that 43 ♖d3 c5! is unclear.

The game concluded :

43	...	♘xb4
44	♗xh7	♘c2+
45	♔f2	♖d2+
46	♔g1	♖d1+
47	♔g2	♖d2+
48	♔h3	♔c7

The rook and pawn ending resulting from 48 ... ♖d1 49 ♖b2 ♖h1+ 50 ♔g2 ♖xh6 51 ♖xc2 ♖xh7 52 fxe5 fxe5 53 ♖xc6 is very good for White.

49	fxe5	fxe5
50	♖b2	♖d7
51	♗g8	♘d4
52	h7	♖xh7+
53	♗xh7	c5
54	♗xg6	c4

55	Qf7	c3
56	Rb1	Kb7
57	g4	1-0

Botvinnik – Szilagyi
Amsterdam 1966

1	g3	d5
2	Nf3	c6
3	Qg2	Qg4
4	d3	Nd7
5	h3	Qxf3?!

As usual in such positions, this exchange is not to be recommended, so the retreat 5 ... Qh5 is best.

| 6 | Qxf3 | e5? *(94)* |

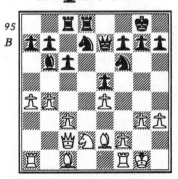

Black follows his unwise voluntary 'sacrifice' of the two bishops with another positional mistake – that of neglecting the squares d5 and f5. 6 ... e6 was called for as now White's King's Indian Attack bishop will have more scope.

7	Nd2	Ngf6
8	e4	dxe4

Otherwise White may open up the position later with exd5 and c4.

| 9 | dxe4 | Qc5 |

10	0-0	We7
11	c3!	0-0?!

Necessary was 11 ... a5, after which White would be better placed, thanks to his bishop pair and white-square control. Now White is able to increase his advantage by expanding on the queenside – often a good idea.

12	b4	Qb6
13	a4!	

Claiming more space and indirectly preparing Nc4 by putting a pawn on b5 before Black does.

13	...	Rfd8
14	Wc2	Rac8
15	Qe2! *(95)*	

When White's king's bishop finds itself on f3 (usually as a result of ... Qxf3 from Black) it is important to remember that the stereotyped retreat to g2 is not necessarily the best course. In this case the a2 - g8 diagonal holds the most promise for the bishop. The reader will notice from other games in this chapter that the h3 - c8 diagonal is also occasionally used.

| 15 | ... | c5? |

Although it does not give away material, Black's blunder allows his opponent a free hand positionally. Chess masters often remark that "good positions play themselves"; Botvinnik's conduct of the rest of the game should help to explain this maxim.

16	b5	♘e8
17	♘c4	♘d6
18	♗g5!	

Not surprisingly the harmonious development of the White pieces facilitates such a tactic. Now 18 ... ♕xg5 19 ♘xd6 followed by ♗c4 leaves Black in dire straits, whilst after 18 ... ♘f6 White can avoid exchanging his knight and instead play ♘e3 - d5. Black is therefore obliged to enhance the power of White's king's bishop with his next move.

18	...	f6
19	♗e3	♘xc4
20	♗xc4+	♔h8
21	a5	♗c7
22	♖fd1	♘f8
23	♕a2!	

The main purpose of this move is to prevent ... ♘e6. The queen will also take over the defence of the a-pawn now that the rooks are about to be exchanged.

23	...	♖xd1+
24	♖xd1	♖d8
25	♖xd8	♗xd8
26	a6!	b6
27	♔g2	(96)

96
B

The removal of the rooks has in no way helped Black, who is powerless to defend against an invasion on the white squares. Botvinnik's next plan is to reverse the present line-up on the a2 - g8 diagonal in order to tie down the potentially troublesome knight. The fact that he can first improve his king's position is indicative of Black's passivity. Indeed, Black is effectively in a lost position.

27	...	♕d7
28	♕e2	♘g6
29	♗b3	♘e7
30	♕c4	h6
31	♕f7	♔h7
32	♗c4	

Almost toying with Black.

32	...	♕d6
33	h4	♕d1
34	♕e8	

Threatening to highlight his total command of the white squares with h5, ♗f7, ♗g6+ and mate. Black's next is tantamount to resignation.

| 34 | ... | f5 |
| 35 | exf5 | ♘xf5 |

| 36 | ♗g8+ | ♔h8 |
| 37 | ♘f7+ | 1-0 |

Note that 5 ... ♗xf3 and 6 ... e5 (rather than 6 ... e6) created considerable white-squared weaknesses in the Black camp. Botvinnik concentrated on these until the end.

6 Black Plays ... d5 and ... ♗f5

1	♘f3	d5
2	g3	♘f6
3	♗g2	c6
4	0-0	♗f5 *(97)*

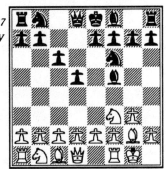

The ... ♗f5 system is similar to ... ♗g4 in that Black avoids blocking in his queen's bishop and develops it on the kingside. Unlike the previous chapter, however, Black is not so well placed to push with ... e5 because there is no pressure against White's king's knight. The c6 – d5 – e6 pawn centre is therefore the best set-up, and this also acts to reduce the range of White's king's bishop.

Once again White has the ♕e1 plan at his disposal to force through e2 – e4. This has the advantage of leaving a rook on f1, which often works out to

be an important factor when White is ready to build up a dangerous kingside attack by throwing forward his f-pawn (there is even a form of attack in which White plays ♔h1 and ♖g1, followed by advancing the g-pawn).

When White prefers a more positional game, then ♖e1 is okay, but with the queen's bishop still on c1 White should be careful if Black has not yet played ... ♘bd7, as the open d-file may mean that multiple exchanges on e4 leave the rook having to cover both e4 and d1. Another reason why Black should not be too hasty with ... ♘bd7 is that an e4 – e5 push from White before Black has castled will chase the king's knight to an unsuitable square.

Since this variation is based around the development of Black's queen's bishop, it is advisable to create a retreat square on h7 in readiness for White's e2 – e4 with the move ... h7 – h6. The h7-square is a good place for the bishop, forcing White to be careful about the c2- and d3-squares.

White has a basic choice of what to do with his own queen's bishop: spend time on an early fianchetto, delay it, or even do without this form of development altogether. The former scheme invites Black to seek counterplay on the queenside with ... a5, threatening the annoying ... a4. It is worth noting here a surprisingly common move order mistake which occurred in Ledger – Levitt, London 1990 *(98)*.

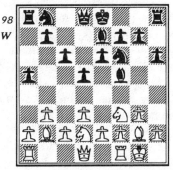

98
W

In the diagram position White seized upon his opponent's careless move order with 9 e4!, the point being 9 ... dxe4 10 dxe4 ⛀xe4 11 ⛀xg7 breaks up Black's kingside. Thus Black had to move his bishop, and White had saved himself the preparatory ♕e1. Note that ... ⛀bd7 instead of ... a5 allows the same response.

Black should avoid also 1 ⛀f3 d5 2 g3 c6 3 ⛀g2 ⛀f5 4 0-0 ⛀f6 5 d3 ⛀bd7 6 ⛀h4!, as in the game Savon – Gligoric, Moscow 1989, when 6 ... ⛀g6 7 e4 dxe4 8 ⛀xg6 hxg6 9 dxe4 e5

10 ⛀d2 ⛀c5 11 a4 0-0 12 ⛀b3 ⛀e7 13 ⛀e3 favoured White. But after 5 ... e6 Black is not worried about his bishop being harassed, as 6 ⛀h4?! ⛀g4 7 h3 ⛀h5 8 g4 ⛀fd7! makes use of the d8 – h4 diagonal. In general, White has a good game against this variation because Black's ostensibly powerful queen's bishop gets locked out of the action, and White seems to find it too easy to develop a dangerous initiative on the kingside.

White Fianchettoes Queenside

Polugayevsky – Addison
Palma Interzonal 1970

1	⛀f3	d5
2	g3	c6
3	⛀g2	⛀f5
4	d3	h6
5	⛀bd2	⛀f6
6	0-0	e6
7	b3	⛀e7
8	⛀b2	0-0
9	♕e1!	

An alternative, but less accurate, way of achieving the e2 – e4 push is by playing 9 ♖e1. However, the idea of ♕e1, e4 and ♕e2 (or e3, ♕e2 and e4) leaves the rook more usefully placed on the f-file, as White will eventually push his f-pawn. It is also important that White keep the e1-square clear so that it will be possible if necessary to play ⛀f3 – e1, both unleashing the f-pawn and defending the c-pawn.

9 ... ♗h7

10 e4 *(99)*

99
B

10 ... a5

As usual, Black must begin active operations on the queenside in order to distract White's attention from the other flank. With his last move Black threatens to cause White problems by continuing with ... a4 - a3 or by a well-timed exchange on b3. Polugayevsky - Planinc, Skopje 1971, followed another path when Black decided to open the d-file with 10 ... dxe4. This worked to White's advantage: 11 dxe4 ♘a6 (Vukic - Miles, Novi Sad 1975, continued 11 ... ♘bd7 12 ♕e2 ♕c7 13 e5 ♘d5 14 ♘e4 ♖fd8, when 15 a3 followed by ♖fd1 would have favoured White) 12 ♕e2 ♘c5 13 ♘e5 ♕c7 14 ♔h1 ♖ad8 15 f4 ♘e8 16 ♖ad1 ♘d6 17 ♕e3! ♘a6 (17 ... ♘d7 18 ♘d3 and 17 ... ♘c8 18 ♕c3! are both bad for Black) 18 a3 ♗f6? (White would also be better after 18 ... ♘b5 19 b4 c5 20 c4 ♘d4 21 b5 ♘b8) 19 g4!

and Black is in danger of being overrun.

11 a4

This is usually the best reaction to ... a5, as 11 a3 invites a future ... a4 which could turn out well for Black.

11 ... ♘a6

Again Black aims to pressure his opponent's queenside with ... ♘b4. Korchnoi - Reshevsky, Amsterdam (match) 1968, saw instead 11 ... ♘bd7 12 ♕e2 ♕b6 13 e5 ♘e8 14 ♗h3! with a slight advantage to White. After 14 ... ♘c7 15 ♔h1 ♖ae8 16 ♘h4 f6 17 exf6 ♗xf6 18 ♗xf6 ♖xf6 Black had succeeded in eliminating White's powerful e-pawn, but 19 f4 ♕c5 20 ♘df3 still left White better thanks to his renewed control of the e5-square.

Bringing the other knight to d7 with 11 ... ♘fd7 leads to Vukic - Buljovcic, below.

12 ♕e2

A similar position would arise after 12 e5 ♘d7 13 ♕e2 ♘b4 14 ♘e1. In the game Vladimirov - Kharitonov, USSR 1977, White developed a kingside attack after 14 ... ♕b6 15 ♔h1 ♕a6 16 f4 ♖fe8 17 ♖f3 c5 18 g4.

12 ... ♘b4

13 ♘e1 ♘d7

In Quinteros - Spiridonov, Cienfuegos 1972, Black unwisely underestimated White's kingside attacking chances. The game went 13 ... ♕b6?! 14 ♔h1 ♖fd8 15 e5! ♘d7 16 f4 ♕a6 17 g4!

♖e8 18 ♕f2 ♗f8 19 ♕g3 c5 20 f5, and Black was in trouble. Also possible is 13 ... dxe4, although this gives White use of c4 for his queen's knight. Addison's move is designed to lure the white e-pawn forward whence it will be challenged with ... f6.

14	f4	♗f6
15	e5	♗e7
16	g4	

With his queenside under no immediate pressure White may now go on the offensive.

16	...	♖e8
17	♔h1	

Tucking the king safely in the corner is always a good idea in positions of this nature.

17	...	f6? *(100)*

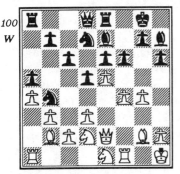

Perhaps this is a natural reaction when faced with a potential pawn storm, although counter-attacking on the queenside was called for. Gligoric has recommended 17 ... b5, while Kotov preferred 17 ... c5 followed by ... ♕c7 (to defend the b-pawn), ... d4 and ... ♘d5. In both cases White has the better practical chances since

he is attacking the king.

An important feature of the King's Indian Attack which the reader should bear in mind is that positions arise frequently which have White attacking on the kingside and Black on the queenside. Not surprisingly, therefore, this makes White's task easier as inaccurate defence on Black's part will have more serious consequences.

Returning to the diagram position we see that play revolves – as is often the case – around the e5-square. White's firm grip accentuates his advantage.

18	♘df3	fxe5
19	♘xe5	♘xe5
20	♗xe5	c5
21	♖d1	

A prophylactic measure designed to give Black second thoughts about pushing with ... c4 (which could have been the answer to 21 ♘f3) to open up the queen's bishop's h7 – b1 diagonal.

21	...	♘c6
22	♘f3	♘xe5
23	♘xe5	

It is generally indicative that things have gone well for White when he has a host of pieces ready to occupy the e5-square.

23	...	♕c7
24	♕e3!	

Preparing to continue his kingside attack with 25 g5.

24	...	♗d6

25	♖de1	♖f8
26	h4!	♔h8
27	♕g3	♖a6

Indirectly defending the e-pawn.

28	g5	♖b6
29	♗h3!	♕e7?

Exchanging with 29 ... ♗xe5 30 ♖xe5 ♕f7 would have at least relieved some of the pressure which White has built up. Now Polugayevsky cleverly turns his initiative and positional advantage into a won game.

30	gxh6	gxh6
31	♘g6+	♗xg6
32	♖xe6!	*(101)*

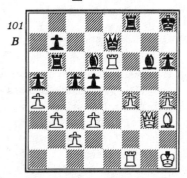

101
B

The point – White wins a pawn and activates his rook (also pinning the ♘d6) before recapturing on g6. Now 32 ... ♗xf4?? 33 ♖xe7 ♗xg3 34 ♖xf8 is mate, so Black complicates things by throwing another piece into the fray.

32	...	♖xf4
33	♕xf4!	♗e4+

The only try, as both 33 ... ♗xf4 34 ♖xe7 and 33 ... ♕xe6 34 ♕xh6+ are final.

34	♖xe4	dxe4
35	♕xh6+	♕h7

Not 35 ... ♔g8 36 ♗e6+.

36	♕f6+	♕g7
37	♕d8+	♔h7
38	♕xb6	♕g3
39	♕xb7+	♔h6
40	♖f6+	♔h5
41	♕h7	mate

It is evident that Black must be careful in this variation. White's over-protection of e5 gave him a positional advantage which made the execution of an attack quite easy.

Vukic – Buljovcic
Novi Sad 1975

1	♘f3	d5
2	g3	c6
3	♗g2	♘f6
4	b3	

Playing an early b3 has the advantage of keeping Black guessing as to what White will do with the centre pawns.

4	...	♗f5
5	♗b2	e6
6	0-0	♗e7
7	d3	h6
8	♘bd2	0-0
9	♕e1	♗h7
10	e4	a5
11	a4	

Despite a different move order we have the same position at this point as in the previous game. Here Black decides to hold back the development of his queen's knight rather than play ... ♘b8 - a6 -

b4. Instead, he intends to advance his c-pawn after White has played e4 – e5.

11 ...   ♘fd7

11 ... c5?! is premature because White still has the possibility of exd5. Indeed in the game Vukic – Chekhov, Banja Luka 1976, Black followed up 11 ... c5 12 ♘e5 with another mistake: 12 ... ♘fd7? (12 ... ♘bd7 13 f4 is better for White) 13 ♘xd7 ♕xd7 14 exd5 exd5 15 ♗xd5! ♕xd5 16 ♕xe7 ♘c6 17 ♕h4, and White had safely won a pawn.

12 ♕e2

Vacating e1 for the knight.

12 ...   ♗f6

Black continues with his plan, which White is happy to go along with.

13 e5!

White should preserve his queen's bishop for future attacking purposes unless an exchange helps him.

13 ...   ♗e7

14 ♘e1

A thematic and sound retreat. The more active looking 14 ♘d4 helps Black accelerate his queenside play: 14 ... ♕b6 15 f4 c5! 16 ♘4f3 c4+.

14 ...   c5

Black prepares to bring his knight to c6 to better observe the centre and put the d4-square under more pressure. This is a good plan because White had to withdraw support of d4 in order to free his f-pawn.

15 f4   ♘c6

16 ♔h1   ♕c7 *(102)*

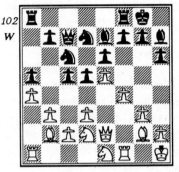

17 c4?!

Just as Black must pay great attention to matters on the kingside, White should do likewise on the other flank. Understandably, White is right to seriously consider his opponent's possibilities on the queenside and not ignore them, but his reaction here is not at all necessary. It is better to put one's faith in the solidity of the queenside and continue with the kingside build-up with 17 ♘df3 and g3 – g4.

Now Black can use the d-file to hit the d-pawn, which is no longer defended by the c-pawn.

17 ...   dxc4!

18 bxc4

Not 18 dxc4 ♘d4! when White stands worse.

18 ...   ♖ad8

19 ♗e4

White eliminates the long-range queen's bishop and consequently reduces the pressure on his d-pawn.

19 ...   ♗xe4

20 ♘xe4

Another result of this exchange is White's influential knight outpost on e4, as well as removing a useful kingside defender.

20 ... ♘db8?

Black chooses a faulty plan, which he will not get the time to realise. After ... ♘d4 he hopes to place his remaining knight on c6. However, 20 ... ♘b6 would have led to a balanced game after 21 ♖f3 ♘b4 followed by ... ♕c6, threatening the a4-pawn and occupying White's weakened h1 – a8 diagonal.

21 g4!

White sets his pawn-roller in motion.

21 ... ♘d4
22 ♗xd4!

The white knights are the superior pieces in this position, and Black will be too busy trying to hold his kingside together to profit from his grip on the dark squares.

22 ... cxd4
23 g5!

White's attack is beginning to look very dangerous.

23 ... hxg5
24 ♕h5! *(103)*

A look at the diagram position reveals a sorry lack of pieces which can come to the aid of Black's king.

Of course 24 ... gxf4?? now would be suicidal as White is ready to bring a rook to the g-file: 25 ♘f6+! ♗xf6 (25 ... gxf6 26 ♖g1 mate) 26 exf6 ♘d7 27 fxg7 ♔xg7 28 ♖g1+ ♔f6 29 ♕g5 mate. Nor does 24 ... f6? offer a chance of survival as 25 exf6 ♗xf6 26 fxg5 will soon lead to White playing g5 – g6.

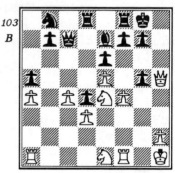

24 ... ♘d7
25 ♘f3 ♖fe8

25 ... f6? is met by 26 fxg5! ♘xe5 27 g6.

26 ♘exg5 ♗xg5
27 ♘xg5 ♘f8

Black has succeeded in defending as well as possible, but White has two rooks in reserve which guarantee victory.

28 ♖f3! ♘g6
29 ♖g1 ♔f8
30 ♘xf7! ♕xf7
31 ♖xg6 1–0

32 f5 is coming, and the black king cannot run away with 31 ... ♔e7 because of 32 ♕g5+.

After Black failed to capitalise on the imprecise 17 c4? he was subjected to a classic kingside attack typical of this variation.

White Plays an Early e4

In the following games White dispenses with a queen-side fianchetto and works for quicker action in the centre. This may not be the type of line for those players who like to develop their pieces, but the time saved could prove useful to White.

Vaganian – Sveshnikov
Sochi 1980

1	♘f3	d5
2	g3	♘f6
3	♗g2	c6
4	0-0	♗f5
5	d3	e6
6	♘bd2	

An unusual development of the queen's bishop was seen in Powell – Peters, USA 1976. White tried the provocative and original 6 ♗f4!? and Black gamely countered by preparing ... g5. The game continued: 6 ... h6 7 ♘bd2 ♘bd7 8 ♕e1 g5!? 9 e4! with a complicated battle which turned out in White's favour after 9 ... dxe4? (better is 9 ... ♗g6 10 ♘e3 ♗g7!, when it is Black who has a strong bishop on the a1 – h8 diagonal) 10 dxe4 ♗g4 (10 ... ♗g6 11 ♘e3 ♘xe4 12 ♘xe4 ♗xe4 13 ♗d4!; or 11 ... ♗xe4 12 ♘xe4 ♘xe4 13 ♗xa7 ♘xg3 14 ♗d4) 11 ♗e3.

6	...	♗e7
7	♕e1 *(104)*	
7	...	h6

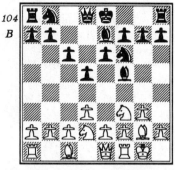

| 8 | e4 | ♗h7 |

Black exchanged on e4 in Reshevsky – Smyslov, USSR vs Rest of the World 1970. There followed (8 ... dxe4) 9 dxe4 ♗h7 10 ♕e2 ♘bd7 11 e5 (it is too late to change plans and go for a queenside fianchetto as Black can aim at the e-pawn: 11 b3?! ♘c5 12 ♗b2 ♘xe4 13 ♗xf6 ♗xf3 14 ♗xe7 ♗xe2 15 ♗xd8 ♖xd8, so 12 e5 is forced, but 12 ... ♘d5 favours Black) 11 ... ♘d5 12 ♘e4 ♘c5 13 ♘xc5 ♗xc5 14 ♘d2! ♕c7 (not 14 ... ♗xc2 15 ♕c4!) 15 a3 0-0. Now White should have played 16 ♔h1! followed by f4, when Black is under pressure.

| 9 | ♘e5!? | |

White clears the way for the charge of the f-pawn. This active strategy is more suitable here because White is able to use the time it would have taken to play b3 and ♗b2 to throw his kingside pawns forward. 9 ♕e2 transposes to the following game, Gutman – Lejnov, but Vaganian hopes that leaving the queen on e1 will prove useful since the subse-

quent advance of the f- and g-
pawns will provide an entry to
the kingside by opening the e1-
h4 diagonal.

	9	...	♘bd7
	10	♘xd7	♘xd7

Not 10 ... ♕xd7? 11 e5 when
Black's knight lacks a good
square.

	11	f4	0-0
	12	♔h1	a5

Black reacts with an assault
of his own.

	13	g4	a4?!

Consistent but not correct.
Better was 13 ... dxe4 14 dxe4
♘c5, limiting White to a slight
edge.

	14	f5	a3
	15	b3	♖e8
	16	♖b1	exf5
	17	gxf5	♕a5
	18	exd5	cxd5
	19	♕g3	♗b4
	20	♘f3	♔h8 (105)

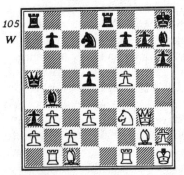

White threatened 21 ♗xh6.
Also insufficient is 20 ... ♗xf5
21 ♗xh6 ♗g6 22 ♘h4!, e.g. 22 ...
gxh6 23 ♘xg6 fxg6 24 ♕xg6+
♔h8 25 ♖f7.

A cursory glance at the
diagram position suggests that
Black's dark-square control
gives him a comfortable game.
A closer inspection, however,
tells another story. White's
kingside pawn charge has
accomplished more than Black's
efforts on the queenside, and
Vaganian now endeavours to
strip away his opponent's defences.

	21	f6!	♘xf6
	22	♗xh6!	♘h5

Accepting the sacrifice does
not help: 22 ... gxh6 23 ♘e5 ♖e7
(or 23 ... ♖xe5 24 ♕xe5 ♗c3 25
d4) 24 ♖xf6 ♖g8 25 ♕h4! ♖xe5
26 ♖xh6 ♖g7 27 ♖xh7+ ♖xh7 28
♕f6+.

	23	♕g4	♖a6
	24	♘g5!	♗g6

Not 24 ... gxh6?? 25 ♘xf7
mate; or 24 ... ♖xh6?? 25 ♘xf7+
♔g8 26 ♘xh6+.

	25	♘xf7+	♗xf7
	26	♗xg7+!	

White sacrifices a piece to
break into his opponent's kingside.

	26	...	♘xg7
	27	♖xf7	♗f8
	28	♖bf1	♕c5
	29	b4	♕d6

Not 29 ... ♕xb4 30 ♖xf8+
♕xf8 31 ♖xf8+ ♖xf8 32 ♕h3+!
♔g8 33 ♗xd5+.

	30	♖xg7!	♗xg7
	31	♕h5+	♕h6
	32	♕xe8+	♔h7
	33	♗xd5	

The King's Indian Attack
bishop comes into play, threat-

ening two deadly checks.

33	...	♕h3
34	♗e4+	♔h6
35	♖g1	1-0

Black cannot defend against the threat of 36 ♖g6+ without suffering a decisive loss of material.

Gutman – Lejnov
Israel 1980

1	♘f3	d5
2	g3	♘f6
3	♗g2	♗f5
4	0-0	c6

Also possible is 4 ... e6 5 d3 h6 6 ♘bd2 ♗e7 7 ♕e1 0-0 8 e4 ♗h7 9 ♕e2 c5!?, when Black has dispensed with ... c6 in readiness for a quick queenside assault. Plachetka - Yusupov, Lucerne Olympiad 1982, continued 10 b3?! ♘c6 11 ♗b2 c4! 12 bxc4 (12 exd5 cxd3 and 12 dxc4 dxe4 13 ♘e5 ♘d4 14 ♕d1 e3! are both very good for Black) 12 ... dxe4 13 dxe4 ♕c7 with a comfortable game for Black.

However, 10 ♘e5 is more likely to highlight the deficiency of the ... c5 idea (which does go against the solid nature of the ... ♗f5 lines). After 10 ♘e5 ♘c6 11 ♘xc6 leaves Black with potentially weak doubled pawns and 10 ... ♘bd7 11 ♘xd7 ♕xd7 12 e5 ♘e8 13 ♘f3 ♘c7 14 ♗f4 gives White the advantage thanks to his over-protection of the e5-pawn and good prospects of a kingside attack.

5	d3	h6
6	♘bd2	e6
7	e3	(106)

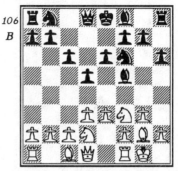

If White intends to put his queen on e2 then this method of forcing through e4 is fine. Of course the interesting try which was successful for White in the previous game is equally possible.

7	...	♗e7
8	♕e2	0-0
9	e4	♗h7
10	♔h1!?	

Introducing a seemingly blunt but effective attacking plan of playing ♖g1 and pushing the g-pawn.

| 10 | ... | ♘bd7 |

Too passive. A vigorous queenside counter-attack is called for such as 10 ... a5! 11 e5 ♘fd7 12 ♖g1 c5! 13 ♘f1 ♕c7 14 g4 ♘c6 15 ♗f4 ♘d4! 16 ♘xd4 cxd4 with enough pressure to at least distract White from his kingside mission.

| 11 | e5 | ♘e8 |
| 12 | ♖g1 | ♘c7 |

Supporting the e-pawn in preparation for a challenge

against White's advanced e-pawn with ... f6. White anticipates this thrust.

13	g4!	f6
14	exf6	♗xf6
15	♘f1	♕e7
16	g5!	*(107)*

107
B

A temporary pawn sacrifice which enables White to further open the g–file for his rook.

16	...	hxg5
17	♗h3	♗f5
18	♘xg5	♗xg5
19	♗xg5	♕f7
20	♗xf5	♕xf5

Black underestimates the danger he faces on the g–file. Recapturing with the pawn is an improvement, and after 20 ... exf5! 21 ♘g3 ♖ae8, White's best is to take a slight endgame advantage with 22 ♕h5 ♘e6 23 ♕xf7+ ♖xf7 24 ♖ae1.

Now White can keep the position sufficiently closed to maintain dangerous threats against the black king, without the worry of his opponent having counterplay down the e-file.

| 21 | f4 | d4 |

22	♘g3	♕d5+
23	♖g2	♖f7
24	♘e4?!	

It is natural that White would like to occupy the newly available e4-square with his knight, although 24 ♖g1 causes Black more immediate problems.

| 24 | ... | e5 |
| 25 | f5! | ♖xf5 |

The pawn must be removed as the threat of f5 – f6 is difficult to prevent.

| 26 | ♗h6 | ♖f7 |
| 27 | ♖ag1 | ♘e8! |

The most accurate defensive resource. The alternative 27 ... ♘e6 results in an even better game for White after 28 ♖g6! ♘df8 29 ♖6g4.

| 28 | ♖g5! | |

Intending to triple on the g-file with ♕g2.

| 28 | ... | ♘df6 |

If Black escapes the pin on the g-file with 28 ... ♔f8 White makes another: 29 ♖xg7! ♖xg7 30 ♕g2 ♕g8 31 ♗xg7+ ♘xg7 32 ♕h3 ♔e8 33 ♕g4. White is clearly much better, but Black is surviving.

29	♕g2	♘xe4
30	dxe4	♕d7
31	♕g3!	

We will soon see why this clever move is preferable to 31 ♖xe5 ♘c7 32 ♖g5 ♘e6 33 ♖g6 ♖e8 with good drawing chances for Black.

| 31 | ... | ♕e7 |
| 32 | ♕b3! | *(108)* |

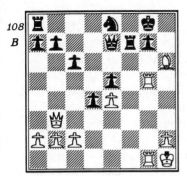

Gutman uses his queen to full effect. Thanks to this second pin the threat is 33 ♖xg7+! ♘xg7 34 ♖xg7+ ♔f8 35 ♖xf7+.

32 ...   ♔f8

There is no escape the other way: 32 ... ♔h8 33 ♗xg7! ♘xg7 34 ♕h3+ ♔g8 35 ♖h5! threatening 36 ♖h8+.

33 ♖h5!   ♔g8

Accepting the poisonous bishop with 33 ... gxh6 allows 34 ♖xh6 ♕d7 35 ♕b4+ (35 ... ♖e7 36 ♖h8+ ♔f7 37 ♖h7+ ♔f8 38 ♖f1+ and ♖xe7).

34 ♗xg7!

White is ready to make the final breakthrough.

34 ...   ♘xg7
35 ♕h3   ♖ff8

Or 35 ... ♖f4 36 ♖h8+ ♔f7 37 ♕h7!.

36 ♖h8+   ♔f7
37 ♖xg7+!   ♔xg7
38 ♕h7+   ♔f6
39 ♕f5+   1-0

39 ... ♔g7 40 ♖h7+ ♔g8 41 ♕g6+.

White announced his intentions of attacking down the g-file as early as his tenth move. Instead of immediately instigating a thematic queenside counter, Black rather unwisely elected to try and match his opponent on the kingside.

In the following game Black delays castling in order to speed up the generation of a queenside attack.

Smyslov – Miles
England 1975

1	♘f3	♘f6
2	g3	d5
3	♗g2	c6
4	0-0	♗f5
5	d3	h6
6	♘bd2	e6
7	♕e1	♗e7
8	e4	♗h7
9	♕e2	♕c7!?

An interesting, if not completely sound, continuation. Black delays castling and looks to the queenside for activity in anticipation of Smyslov closing the centre with e5.

Keene - Zuidema, England 1972, saw Black adopt a policy of castling kingside and then pushing his f- and g-pawns forward! That game went 9 ... 0-0 10 e5 ♘fd7 11 ♖e1 c5 12 ♘f1 ♘c6 13 h4 ♖c8 14 ♗f4 ♖e8 15 ♘1h2 f5!? (15 ... ♗f8! is sensible) 16 c4?! (Keene gives 16 h5 as an improvement, although it is difficult to see that Black's next will be more useful than weakening) 16 ... g5 17 ♗e3 d4 18

♗c1 g4 19 ♘d2 ♘dxe5 (19 ...
♘cxe5 20 ♘b3! threatens both
♗xb7 and ♗xh6) 20 ♗xc6 ♘xc6
21 ♕xe6+ ♔g7 22 ♘b3 and
White stands slightly better.

10	e5	♘fd7
11	♖e1	c5
12	c4 *(109)*	

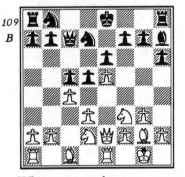

White must take care not to
succumb to a queenside pawn
avalanche, especially with
Black's queen's bishop sitting
on the b1 - h7 diagonal. It is
true that the d-pawn is now a
weakness, but if Black manages
to get ... c4 in the pawn will be
weaker still after ... cxd3, and
dxc4 from White opens the
diagonal still further and makes
c2 a target.

Establishing a pawn on c4
helps form a good blockade
which is designed to keep
Black albeit temporarily at bay
while White builds up an attack
on the kingside.

12	...	d4
13	♘f1	♘c6
14	♗d2	

Preventing ... ♘b4.

| 14 | ... | ♖b8 |

15	g4	b5

Another idea is 15 ... a6 to
meet cxb5 with ...axb5, after
which Black will play for ... c4.
However, Black appreciates the
importance of a quick counter
to White's kingside build-up.

16	cxb5	♖xb5
17	b3	a5
18	♘g3	0-0

Black needs both rooks to
continue with his queenside
attack, and his king is no safer
in the centre than it is on g8.

19	g5!	hxg5
20	♗xg5	♖fb8

20 ... ♗xg5 21 ♘xg5 ♘cxe5 22
♘xh7 ♔xh7 23 ♕e4+ ♔h8 (23 ...
♘g6 24 ♕c6!) 24 f4 is good for
White.

21	♗xe7	♘xe7
22	♖ac1!	

The threat of ♘xd4 forces
the black queen to vacate c7.

22	...	♕d8
23	♘g5	♗g6
24	h4	a4

Active play from both sides.
Nevertheless, White's assort-
ment of pieces on the kingside
make his attack considerably
easier to conduct.

25	bxa4	♖b2
26	♕f3	♖xa2
27	♗h3	♖a3
28	h5!	♖xd3
29	♕g2!	

From here the queen can
oversee events without ob-
structing the minor pieces.

| 29 | ... | ♖bb3 *(110)* |

29 ... ♖xg3 does not alleviate

Black's problems: 30 ♕xg3 ♗xh5 31 ♘xe6! fxe6 32 ♗xe6+ ♔h7 33 ♕h3. Instead Black continues down the path of counter-attack, hoping for 30 hxg6 ♘xg6 with dangerous compensation for the sacrificed piece.

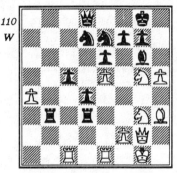

110
W

30 ♘xe6!

Uncompromising and best, resulting in simplifications which are very favourable for White.

30	...	fxe6
31	♗xe6+	♔f7
32	♗xf7+	♔xf7
33	e6+	♔g8
34	exd7	♕xd7
35	♘e4	

Threatening 36 ♘xc5 and 36 ♘f6+.

35	...	♕h3!
36	♖xc5!	

Not falling for the trap by 36 ♘xc5? ♖g3!.

36	...	♕xg2+
37	♔xg2	♖b7
38	♘g5!	♖c3

Black cannot defend his d-pawn, knight and back rank simultaneously (White threatened 39 ♖c8+! ♘xc8 40 ♖e8 mate).

39	♖d5!	♖c8

Of course not 39 ... ♘xd5?? 40 ♖e8 mate.

40 ♖xd4

And White eventually converted his material advantage into the full point.

Smyslov's handling of the attack, under pressure from Miles's energetic retaliation, is a good example of how one can generate threats on the king-side - even when facing an adversary who recognises that quiet play is no answer to White's build-up.

7 King's Indian Reversed

1	♘f3	c5
2	g3	d5
3	♗g2	♘c6
4	0-0	*(111)*

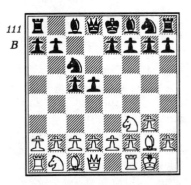

When Black pushes with both ... c5 and ... d5 the adversaries reverse roles and White is playing a King's Indian Defence with an extra tempo. Of course, White should be happy to go along with this, especially as the King's Indian is such a reputable defence. Nevertheless, Black often volunteers to allow White this luxury, and the most popular choice is to fianchetto the king's bishop, as in the first three games. The other two see Black adopting a version of the Classical Variation.

Fianchetto System

Hickl – Lev
Bern Zonal 1990

1	g3	c5
2	♗g2	♘c6
3	e4	g6
4	d3	♗g7
5	♘f3	♘f6
6	0-0	0-0
7	c3	d5 *(112)*

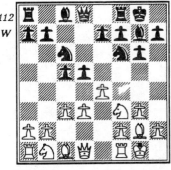

With this move Black adopts the popular fianchetto system which is used by White against the King's Indian Defence. Not surprisingly, the extra tempo helps White here, but Black's set-up is logical and gives a reasonable game. The more conservative 7 ... d6 would result in a transposition to the

Sicilian Defence.

8 ♘bd2 e5

One of several alternatives. Instead, the game Plachetka – Pribyl, Czechoslovakia 1974, saw an attempt to cramp White with 8 ... d4. After 9 cxd4 cxd4 10 a4 e5 11 ♘c4 White stood better, and on 11 ... ♘e8 he used the extra tempo to undertake a queenside offensive with 12 b4!. Such a push can be excellent for White, and the reader should be on the lookout for this active possibility in related positions, particularly when Black has ambitiously advanced his central pawns.

8 ... ♗g4?! is not a good plan for Black, either. Lutikov – Bagirov, Alma-Ata 1969 continued 9 exd5! ♘xd5 10 h3 ♗d7 11 ♘b3 b6 12 d4!, when White's firm control of the centre left him much better.

9 ♖e1

Expansion on the queenside is another plan available to White. Petrosian – Teschner, Stockholm Interzonal 1962, continued 9 a3, aiming to advance the b-pawn. Of course, Black can prevent b2 – b4 with 9 ... a5, but White then happily gives back a tempo with 10 a4, leaving Black's queenside weak (particularly the squares b5 and b6). Consequently, the game went (after 9 a3) 9 ... h6 10 b4 cxb4 11 axb4 b5 12 ♗a3 ♖e8 13 ♕c2 ♗g4 14 ♘b3, when White had a slight pull on the queen-

side.

Popovic – Kirov, Wroclaw 1979, continued instead 9 a4 h6 10 a5!? dxe4 (10 ... ♘xa5? 11 ♘xe5! 11 dxe4 ♕e6 12 ♕e2 ♕c7 13 a6! b6, when White eventually made use of b7 by playing ♘c4 – d6 – b7.

9 ... h6

Black often makes this precautionary move in order to deny his opponent the use of the g5-square, as a future ♗g5 or ♘g5 could undermine Black's control of d5. The space-gaining 9 ... d4 transposes to the game Yap – Bany, Hungary 1986. White immediately sought an initiative on the queenside with 10 cxd4 cxd4 11 ♘c4 ♘e8 12 ♕b3 ♘d6 13 ♗g5 ♗f6 14 ♗xf6 ♕xf6 15 ♘xd6 ♕xd6 16 ♖ec1. Black has problems completing his development, and the passive 16 ... ♖b8 was answered by the thematic 17 ♕d5! ♕f6 18 b4!, when 18 ... ♘xb4 19 ♕xe5 left Black with a weak d-pawn and an inactive game.

10 a4

An almost automatic reaction in many variations. White intends to use c4 as a useful post for his queen's knight, so it is necessary to put a stop to a harassing ... b5 from Black.

10 ... ♖e8

Bringing more support to his e-pawn, which is about to come under pressure from White's pieces after the following central exchange.

11	exd5	♘xd5
12	♘c4 *(113)*	

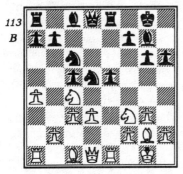

113
B

Although Black enjoys a space advantage his chances of finding a constructive plan are somewhat limited. One policy is to calmly wait and see how White will continue, making sure not to make any structural weaknesses. However, White's game is a little easier to play. He has a definite, albeit minuscule pull on both sides of the board, and his king's bishop - unlike Black's - resides on an open diagonal.

12	...	♘b6!?

An interesting alternative to 12 ... ♗f5, as in Wade – Browne, Hastings 1972/73. Rather than give White a choice of operations, Black challenges his opponent's formidable knight, forcing either a retreat or a relieving exchange.

13	♘e3	

White wisely keeps his piece, consequently retaining the tension.

13	...	♘a5

Black seeks to effectively neutralise White's conventional grip of c4, but at the cost of granting the first player another outpost.

14	♕c2	c4
15	dxc4	♘bxc4
16	♖d1	♕c7
17	♘d5	♕b8

In return for the relinquishing of c4, which now belongs to a black knight, White has command of the d-file and an unchallenged knight on d5. It will also become apparent that White continues to have a mild initiative on both sides of the board, and Hickl now steps up the pace.

18	♘h4	♔h7

With the black pieces over on the queenside Black realises that White's last move did indeed threaten to shatter his kingside with the sacrifice ♘xg6, but now the f7-pawn is left undefended, and White cleverly uses a timely queenside expansion to shift his queen to the a2 - g8 diagonal.

19	b4	♘c6
20	♕a2	♘d6

Not 20 ... ♘b6? 21 ♘xb6 axb6 22 ♕xf7.

21	b5	♘a5
22	♗a3	♘ac4
23	♗b4	

Black has renewed his occupation of c4, while White has managed to push his b-pawn menacingly up the board.

23	...	♗g4
24	♖e1	a5

25	♗xd6	♞xd6
26	b6 *(114)*	

Despite the attempts to curtail his queenside aggression, White has nevertheless succeeded in making tremendous progress on that flank. Moreover, the versatile queen's knight - which soon found a good home after being evicted from c4 - is ready to jump into c7, winning the exchange. Thus Black is reduced to giving up his useful light-squared bishop, leaving yet another mighty white piece to oversee on d5.

26	...	♗e6
27	♕c2	♗xd5
28	♗xd5	♕d8
29	c4	♕xb6

Black takes the proffered pawn and hopes for the best; a good decision in view of the threatened push c4 - c5.

30	c5	♕c7
31	♖ac1	♞c8

Unfortunately for Black 31 ... ♖ac8 32 ♕b1, or 31 ... ♖ec8 32 ♕b3 would leave his position overloaded.

| 32 | f4! | |

For the invested pawn White has a commanding position with a powerful grip on the white squares. He now threatens f4 - f5, aiming at the weak g6-pawn.

32	...	f5

Preventing the aforementioned advance and also removing the f-pawn from the line of fire of White's bishop, enabling ... ♞e7 to be played.

33	♕c4	

It is interesting to look at the movements of the white queen thus far. Persistent pressure on both the b1 - h7 and a2 - g8 diagonals has reaped considerable rewards.

33	...	♞e7
34	♗f7	♖f8
35	♕e6	♖a6 *(115)*

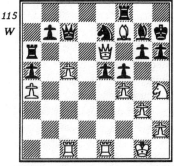

Black develops his rook on his third rank in order to defend the g6-pawn. Since this is the pawn which is holding Black's position together, White manages to remove it by blocking the path of the defending rook.

| 36 | c6! | ♖xc6 |

37	♖xc6	bxc6
38	♗xg6+	♘xg6
39	♕xg6+	♔h8
40	♘xf5	♕f7

With his kingside crumbling Black puts his hopes in a rook and pawn ending.

41	♕xg7+	♕xg7
42	♘xg7	♔xg7
43	♖xe5	♖c8
44	♖c5!	

Not 44 ♖xa5 c5. Instead, White gives himself time to bring his king over to the queenside, as Black cannot defend both his a- and c-pawns simultaneously. White's kingside pawns have remained intact and will be able to help each other advance. As will be seen, this factor gives White a decisive advantage.

44	...	♔f6
45	♔f2	♔e6
46	♔e3	♔d6
47	♖xa5	c5

Black's only hope lies in pushing his c-pawn, so White first monitors the queenside before turning his attentions to the other wing.

48	♔d3	♔d5
49	♖a7	

White heads for the weak h-pawn, inviting Black to make his own, less dangerous, invasion.

49	...	♖b8
50	♔c3	♖e8
51	♖d7+!	

White takes advantage of the fact that the black king is obliged to stay with the c-pawn, making a stop en route to h7 which forces Black to lose time.

51	...	♔c6
52	♖h7	♖e3+
53	♔d2	♖a3
54	♖xh6+	♔d5
55	f5	

The capture of the h-pawn has opened the door for White's pawns to begin the race to the eighth rank.

55	...	♖a2+
56	♔c3	♖a3+
57	♔b2	♖xa4
58	h3	

Preparing g3 – g4.

58	...	♖e4
59	g4	♖f4
60	f6	♔c4

Or 60 ... ♔e6 61 g5, when Black has no way of stopping all three white pawns.

61	g5	♖f2+
62	♔c1	♔d3
63	♖h8	♖f1+
64	♔b2	♖f2+
65	♔a3	

The white king no longer needs to block the opposing pawn.

65	...	c4
66	g6!	1-0

Black went to considerable lengths to nip White's queenside play in the bud, failed, and then saw his kingside succumb to an attack.

In the next game Black chooses a more ambitious continuation than the Symmetrical.

**Weinstein – Westerinen
Budapest 1976**

1	♘f3	♘f6
2	g3	g6
3	♗g2	♗g7
4	0-0	0-0
5	d3	d5
6	♘bd2	c5

Apart from the alternative 6 ... ♘c6 (see Chapter 8), Black has occasionally tried 6 ... d4 in this position, but the advance appears somewhat illogical as it hands over the c4-square to White's queen's knight. The game Hug – Wahls, Bern Zonal 1990, saw White immediately accept the positional gift with 7 ♘c4 c5 8 a4 ♘d5 9 ♘fd2. After 9 ... ♘c6 10 e4 Black was obliged to play 10 ... dxe3 (otherwise White has gained too much time), when 11 fxe3 b6 12 ♕f3 ♗e6 13 ♘e4 left White much better.

7	e4	♘c6
8	c3	h6

A common move, simply planning to develop the queen's bishop on e6 without having to be concerned about a future harassing ♘g5.

9 ♖e1

An option worth considering is 9 exd5, avoiding lines in which Black plays ... dxe4.

9 ... ♗e6 *(116)*

Black decides to do without ... e5.

It is a matter of taste whether Black makes the cent-ral pawn exchange ... dxe4, or allows White to play exd5, although this game does suggest that the former plan at least offers Black more stability. 9 ... dxe4 occurred in Jansa – Forintos, Athens 1969, when 10 dxe4 ♗e6 11 ♕e2 ♘d7 (intending 12 ♘c4 b5!? 13 ♘e3 b4) would have given Black a reasonable game. Instead, Black played the less circumspect 11 ... ♕a5?!, resulting in a good game for White after 12 a4 ♖fd8 13 ♕b5!.

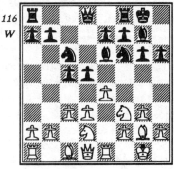

116
W

10 exd5

Also possible is 10 e5 ♘d7 11 d4 cxd4 12 cxd4 - White has an advantage in the centre and on the kingside, but this may be offset by Black's queenside chances and play on the c-file.

10 ... ♘xd5

Weinstein offers 10 ... ♗xd5 as an improvement, yet a move such as 11 ♕c2 leaves White slightly better as Black's king's knight is poorly placed on f6.

11	♘b3!	b6
12	d4!	

The idea of exd5 followed by

♘b3 and d4 is strategically desirable for White. Black often has to defend the c-pawn with ... b6, thus enhancing the power of White's king's bishop, and either a knight or a bolstered pawn on d4 will help White dictate matters in the centre and subsequently the kingside.

12 ... c4

Better than 12 ... cxd4? 13 ♘fxd4 ♘xd4 14 ♘xd4 with a superb position for the first player. With the game move Black hopes to keep the game blocked until he can undermine White's queenside pawns with the advance ... b6 - b5 - b4. Although Black is susceptible to an attack on the kingside or on the white squares, his queen's bishop is at the moment acting as overseer.

13 ♘bd2 ♖c8

13 ... b5 weakens the c5-square, which White can use immediately by playing 14 ♘e4 and then ♘c5. Now White makes a very promising positional exchange sacrifice.

14 ♖xe6!

Not 14 ♘xc4? ♘xc3! 15 bxc3 ♗xc4, although a sound but cautious move is 14 ♘f1, when White has only a minuscule edge.

14 ... fxe6 (117)

Without any pawn breaks to open up the position for his major pieces, Black must wait to put his material advantage

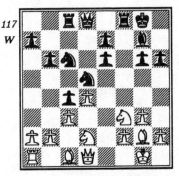

to use. Meanwhile, White has command of the light squares and a few weak black pawns to aim at. White's most accurate continuation now is 15 ♕e2!, threatening 16 ♕xe6+. Then, after 15 ... ♕d7 16 ♘xc4 Black does not have the possibility mentioned in the note to his next move. 15 ♕e2 e5 16 dxe5 b5 17 ♕e4 is also very good for White, whose compensation for the exchange consists of a pawn, a solid position, white-square control and excellent kingside attacking prospects.

However, White chooses a more hazardous follow-up to his sacrifice.

15 ♘xc4!? ♘xd4?!

Grandmaster Westerinen is not a player to shirk complications, but 15 ... b5 deserves consideration here. White could then persevere in swashbuckling style with 16 ♘ce5 ♘xe5 17 ♘xe5 ♗xe5 18 dxe5 ♘xc3! 19 ♕xd8 ♖fxd8 20 bxc3, resulting in an ending in which his two bishops cannot get the better of an active rook: 20 ... ♖d1+ 21

♘f1 ♖xc3 22 ♘b2 ♖xa1 23 ♗xa1 ♖a3 24 ♘xb5 ♖xa2 25 ♘d4 with equality. Consequently, 15 ... b5 16 ♘e3 is best when the position is unclear, so White is better trying 15 ♕e2 as suggested above.

16 ♘xd4 ♖xc4
17 ♕d3!

The tempting 17 ♘xe6? permits 17 ... ♘xc3!, when White has no more than a draw. 18 ♘xd8? ♘xd1 19 ♗d5+ ♔h8 20 ♗xc4 ♖xd8 puts Black in the driving seat, but 18 ♕xd8 ♖xd8 19 ♘xd8 ♘e2+ 20 ♔f1 ♖xc1+ 21 ♖xc1 ♘xc1 draws.

Tricky is (17 ♘xe6 ♘xc3) 18 ♕f1. All of Black's pieces are attacked, yet amazingly 18 ... ♕c8! 19 ♘xf8 ♘e2+! 20 ♕xe2 ♖xc1+ 21 ♖xc1 ♕xc1+ 22 ♗f1 ♔xf8 is completely drawn.

17 ... ♖c8??

The losing move. It was imperative that Black should keep battling in order to have any chance of survival. Once again 17 ... ♘xc3 suggests itself. Play might continue 18 ♕xc4! ♕xd4 19 ♕xe6+ ♔h7 20 bxc3 ♕xc3 (20 ... ♕xf2+ 21 ♔h1 ♗xc3 22 ♗e3! wins for White) 21 ♖b1 ♕c2 22 ♕e4 ♕xf2+ 23 ♔h1 when Black is much worse but still in the game. Perhaps best is 17 ... ♖xd4 18 cxd4 ♔h7, even though White stands considerably better.

18 ♘xe6 ♘xc3

Now this resource is insufficient. Similarly, 18 ... ♘b4 meets

with 19 ♕xg6! ♕d1+ 20 ♔f1 ♖f7 21 ♗xh6! ♕xa1 22 ♗xg7 and Black gets mated.

19 ♘xd8 ♖fxd8
20 ♕e3 1-0

Black does not have enough material for the queen. A wild game, but the tactics after the positional sacrifice were in White's favour.

Dunnington – Gutman
Krumbach 1991

1	♘f3	♘f6
2	g3	g6
3	♗g2	♗g7
4	0-0	0-0
5	d3	d5
6	♘bd2	c5
7	e4	♘c6
8	c3	dxe4

A logical choice. Black immediately clarifies matters in the centre and can now concentrate on completing his development.

9 dxe4 h6 *(118)*

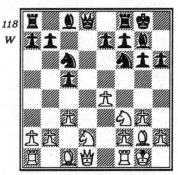

Once again Black prefers to use the e6-square as a home for the queen's bishop, but

unlike the previous game he
does not give White the option
of playing exd5. The plan of ...
b6 followed by ... ♗b7 or ... ♕a6
is also possible, as in Knezevic
– Bertok, Yugoslavia 1977. The
game went 9 ... b6 10 ♕e2 ♘e8
11 ♖d1 ♘c7 12 ♘c4 ♕e8 13 ♘e3
♗a6 14 ♕e1 ♖c8 15 h4! with a
good game for White as Black's
minor pieces on the queenside
are sorely missed on the other
wing.

In Cuderman – Suvalic,
Yugoslavia 1961, Black solved
the problem of where to put
the queen's bishop by exchanging it after 9 ... ♗g4 10 h3 ♗xf3,
but 11 ♕xf3 ♘e5 12 ♕e3 ♘fd7 13
f4 left White with a useful
space advantage as well as the
two bishops.

10   ♕e2   ♗e6
11   h3   ♕a5

Simple development, intending to bring a rook to d8. White
will attempt to keep the queenside and the centre under control and build up pressure on
the kingside. In practice it is
not easy for Black to keep his
pieces out of the way of the
marching enemy pawns.

The alternative 11 ...
♕b6 would transpose after 12 ♘e1 to
Petrosian – Reshevsky, Zurich
Candidates 1953, which continued 12 ... ♖ad8 13 ♔h2 ♘h7 14
f4 ♘a5 15 ♘ef3 ♗d7 16 ♖fe1 ♕c7
17 ♘f1 b6 18 ♘e3. Although a
draw was agreed a dozen
moves later, White has a slight

initiative at this stage.

Note that White does best
to drop his knight back to e1
when preparing to push the
f-pawn. This is because the
weak d3-square must be supported in readiness for Black's
occupation of the d-file. One
example of how White's eager-
ness to start a kingside attack
can lead to a dangerous neglect-
ion of the queenside is (after 11
h3) 11 ... ♕b6 12 ♘h4?! ♖ad8 13
f4 ♖d3!, when 14 ♕xd3 c4+
wins for Black. From e1 the
king's knight also has access to
the often useful c2-square.

12   ♘e1   ♖fd8
13   f4   c4!? *(119)*

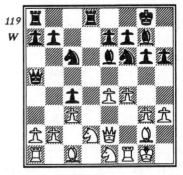

An interesting move typical
of Grandmaster Gutman. Accepting the pawn with 14 ♘xc4
is not wise in view of 14 ... ♕a6
15 b3 ♘a5 when the pin is
uncomfortable.

Now we see the idea behind
11 ... ♕a5: after pushing with ...
c5 – c4 Black further covers his
fourth rank. This presents
White with certain problems if
he wishes to throw forward his

kingside pawns before Black generates sufficient counterplay on the queenside.

Of course, White may simply settle for central play with e4 – e5 followed by ♘e4 and ♗e3, but such a plan does not put Black under as much immediate pressure as the more ambitious game choice.

14	g4	♖ac8
15	♔h1	

Tucking the king in the corner, away from any annoying checks from the black queen.

15	...	g5!?

Black reacts to the vigorous offensive by positional means. Consequently, Black will use the e5-square as an outpost for a blockading knight, thus keeping White's pawn-roller at bay; meanwhile, he hopes to take an initiative on the queenside.

16	f5	

The white pawns must remain united. After 16 fxg5 Black has an excellent position.

16	...	♗d7
17	♘df3	♘e5
18	♘d4	

In return for relinquishing the important e5-square White has received a similarly attractive outpost on d4 for his own knight.

18	...	♗c6
19	♘ec2	*(120)*

White will now complete his development with ♗c1 – d2, perhaps intending to gain space on the queenside with b2 – b4

followed by a2 – a4. Another idea is to transfer the queen's bishop to g3 in order to pressurise the e5-knight and thus invite ... ♘fd7, after which White is free to play ♘c2 – e3 because his e-pawn is sufficiently defended. Black also has to consider White's playing ♘c2 – b4 at some stage, threatening a timely ♘bxc6, so he decides to utilise his development advantage to cut across White's plans.

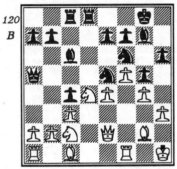

19	...	♘d3
20	♘xc6	♖xc6
21	e5?!	

White seizes the opportunity to make this desired central advance, which in turn permits another black knight to observe the weak f4-square. Perhaps this is too big a price to pay, and White should instead play 21 ♘d4 or 21 ♗e3 (21 ... ♘xb2 22 ♘b4!).

21	...	♘d5
22	♘d4	♖b6
23	e6	♗xd4

Black judges that he has good enough control of the

dark squares to enable the exchange of his king's bishop for White's strong knight.

24 exf7+ ♔f8

Using the enemy pawn as protection rather than potentially exposing the king, e.g. 24 ... ♔xf7 25 cxd4 ♘5f4 26 ♗xf4 ♘xf4 27 ♕xc4+.

25 cxd4 ♘5f4
26 ♗xf4 ♘xf4
27 ♖xf4! gxf4 (121)

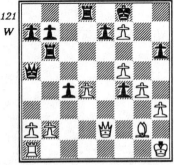

The exchange sacrifice has kept White in the game, thanks to his traditionally powerful bishop and his potentially troublesome pawns. Meanwhile, it is not so easy for Black to successfully defend his c-, e- and f-pawns. Nevertheless, White's compensation should only be sufficient to draw with best play, suggesting that his 21st move was indeed a little too ambitious.

It is important to mention here that both sides - particularly White - had just a few minutes left in which to reach the time control at move forty.

28 ♖e1 ♖d7

29 d5 ♖f6

After 29 ... ♖xb2 White draws with 30 ♕e5, threatening 31 ♕h8+ ♔xf7 32 ♕h7+ etc.

30 ♖d1 ♕b6

Black continues to play safe. Now 31 g5 is useless because the black queen defends the h6-pawn, so that 31 ... ♖xf5 32 ♕h5 ♖xg5 is possible.

31 ♕xc4 ♕c7
32 ♕e2 ♕d6
33 h4

White maintains the pressure before his opponent manages to fully consolidate.

33 ... ♖xf7
34 g5 hxg5
35 ♕h5!

Black suddenly finds himself on the defensive.

35 ... ♔g8

Not 35 ... ♖xf5 36 ♕h8+ ♔f7 37 ♕h7+ when Black must play the awful 37 ... ♔f6.

36 ♖e1! ♕f6
37 hxg5 ♕xf5

37 ... ♕xb2 runs into 38 f6.

38 ♗e4

Forcing Black to simplify into a rook and pawn ending which is good for White.

38 ... ♖h7 (122)

38 ... ♕e5 39 ♗h7+ ♖xh7 40 ♕xh7+ ♔xh7 41 ♖xe5 leads to the same position as the game continuation.

39 ♕xh7+ ♕xh7+

Not 39 ... ♔xh7?? 40 ♗xf5+.

40 ♗xh7+ ♔xh7
41 ♖e5

The smoke has cleared and

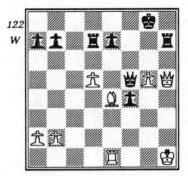

the character of the game has drastically changed. Now it is White who has all the winning chances. Passive play from Black gives White a free hand, so Gutman opts for active defence.

41	...	♖c7
42	♔g2	♖c2+
43	♔f3	♖xb2
44	♔xf4	♖f2+
45	♔g4	♔g6
46	♖xe7	♖xa2
47	♖e6+	♔f7
48	g6+	♔g7
49	♔f5	♖f2+
50	♔e5	♖b2
51	♔f5	♖f2+
52	♔e5	♖b2
53	♖e7+!	

White's d-pawn will win the game. The game finished:

53	...	♔xg6
54	♔e6	♔g5
55	d6	♔f4
56	d7	♖d2
57	♔f7	b5
58	♔e8	b4
59	d8=Q	♖xd8+
60	♔xd8	a5
61	♔c7	b3

62	♔c6	a4
63	♖b7!	1-0

For example, 63 ... ♔d3 64 ♔b5 a3 65 ♔a4 a2 66 ♖xb3+ ♔d2 67 ♖a3.

An exciting game which features the possibilities available to both sides and should also serve as a warning to those players who are prone to overplay the kingside pawn advance.

Classical Variation

In the second half of this chapter we look at typical situations in which Black does not fianchetto his king's bishop.

Vladimirov - Voskanian
USSR 1977

1	♘f3	c5
2	g3	d5
3	♗g2	♘c6
4	0-0	e5
5	d3	♘f6

Black played 5 ... ♘ge7 in the game P. Nikolic - Raicevic, Belgrade 1988. Although this is a sound system for White against the King's Indian Defence, it does not seem to be very good here. The game continued 6 ♘bd2 ♘g6 7 e4 d4 8 a4 ♗e7 9 ♘c4 0-0 10 h4! ♗g4 11 ♕e1 ♕d7 12 ♘fd2 ♗h3 13 h5 ♘h4?, when White calmly refuted Black's play with 14 ♗h1! f5 15 gxh4 ♗xh4 16 ♕e2 ♗xf1 17 ♔xf1 ♗xf2 18 ♔xf2 fxe4+ 19 ♔g1 e3 20 ♘e4 ♖f4 21 ♗g2 ♖af8 22 ♘xc5 ♕c8 23 ♘xe3! dxe3 24 ♗xe3.

One idea behind 5 ... ♘ge7 is that it avoids the system which White uses in this game.

6 ♗g5!? *(123)*

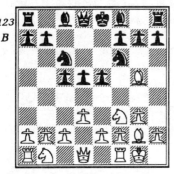

An interesting alternative to 6 ♘bd2, and a tempo up on a line which Black uses in the King's Indian Defence. White's plan is quite simple: to eliminate the f6-knight and fight for control of the white squares, particularly d5 and f5.

6 ... ♗e7
7 ♘fd2

Also playable is 7 ♗xf6 ♗xf6 8 ♘fd2, but 8 ... e4!? may cause White unnecessary problems.

7 ... 0-0

Vladimirov gives 7 ... ♘g8 as a possible way of avoiding any white-square weaknesses. After 8 ♗xe7 ♘gxe7 White's best continuation appears to be 9 c4, aiming to attack the black c-pawn now that Black no longer has a king's bishop with which to defend.

8 ♘c3 ♗e6

9 e4 dxe4

This simplifying exchange makes White's task of dominating d5 easier, so 9 ... d4 is worth consideration, after which 10 ♘e2 ♘d7 is roughly equal, but 10 ♗xf6 ♗xf6 11 ♘d5 is better for White.

10 ♗xf6!? ♗xf6
11 dxe4 ♕d7
12 ♘d5 ♗d8

Taking the knight usually heightens Black's problems in this type of position, e.g. 12 ... ♗xd5 13 exd5 ♘b4 14 ♘e4! with a very good position for White (14 ... ♘xd5? 15 ♘xc5 or 15 ♕xd5 ♕xd5 16 ♘xf6+ and 17 ♗xd5).

13 ♘c4 b5
14 ♘ce3 *(124)*

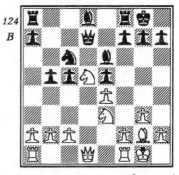

It is easy to see from the diagram that White has appreciated the positional aspects of the ♗g5 idea much better than his opponent. The d5-square is a gaping hole in Black's half of the board, and White even has good chances of seizing f5. As is often the case Black has a territorial advantage on the queenside, but White has such a commanding hold that this will not generate enough compensation for the second player.

14	...	♖b8
15	c3	c4
16	a4	

White spends a move on keeping Black further at bay.

16	...	a6
17	♕h5	

Menacingly taking up position near the black king. White also wants to take advantage of Black's awkward development by moving a rook to the d-file.

17	...	f6
18	♖fd1	♕b7

Black wisely moves his queen out of the line of fire of the opposing rook (White threatened 19 ♘xf6+ and 20 ♖xd7). With his next move White seeks to either exchange Black's good bishop or increase the scope of his own. Whatever course Black chooses, White will accentuate his grip on f5.

19	♗h3	♗f7
20	♕e2	♗b6
21	♘f5	

Threatening 22 ♘d6.

21	...	♗c5
22	♘xf6+!	*(125)*

It was only a matter of time until White converted his overwhelming positional advantage into material gain or a decisive initiative. Black must accept the sacrifice as 22 ... ♔h8 23 ♘d7 is

final.

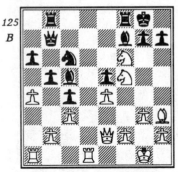

22	...	gxf6
23	♖d7!	♕b6

23 ... ♕xd7 24 ♘h6+ ♔g7 25 ♗xd7 ♔xh6 26 ♗xc6 wins for White.

24	a5!	

A necessary finesse, as 24 ♘h6+ ♔g7 25 ♕h5 ♘e7 is difficult to meet.

24	...	♘xa5
25	♘h6+	♔g7
26	♕h5	♖b7
27	♘f5+	♔h8
28	♕h6	♖g8
29	♖d6!	

White severs the b6 – f6 lifeline (29 ... ♗xd6 30 ♕xf6+ leads to mate next move). Consequently, Black must part with his queen.

29	...	♗xf2+
30	♔g2	♗g6
31	♖xb6	♗xb6
32	♘d6	♖bb8
33	♗f5!	

White's positional superiority combines with a material advantage to produce a won game. The new threat is 34 ♘f7+! ♗xf7 35 ♕xh7 mate.

33	...	♖g7
34	♗xg6	♖xg6
35	♕h3	♘b3
36	♖xa6	♖gg8
37	♕h6	♖g6
38	♖xb6!	*(126)*

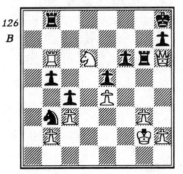

126
B

Often the quickest route to victory after winning a queen is to engineer a situation in which one can sacrifice it back to force almost immediate resignation.

38	...	♖xh6
39	♖xb8+	♔g7
40	♘f5+	♔g6
41	♖g8+	1-0

41 ... ♔f7 42 ♘xh6+ leaves White a rook up, and 41 ... ♔h5 allows 42 g4 mate.

Botvinnik – Pomar
Varna Olympiad 1962

1	g3	d5
2	♘f3	c5
3	♗g2	♘c6
4	d3	e5
5	0-0	*(127)*
5	...	♗d6

Aiming for a kind of reversed Samisch variation. Lazic

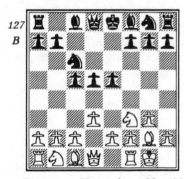

127
B

– Raicevic, Yugoslav Ch 1991, followed a similar course with 5 ... f6. The game continued: 6 e4 (also possible is 6 c4 d4 7 e3 with a reversed Benoni) 6 ... ♘ge7 7 ♘c3 ♗e6 8 ♘h4 d4 9 ♘e2 g5!? 10 ♘f5!? ♘xf5 11 exf5 ♗d5?! (accepting the pawn with 11 ... ♗xf5 was better, when White will try to open up the position) 12 ♘xd5 ♕xd5 13 g4 h5!? 14 gxh5 ♖xh5 15 ♘f4 exf4 16 ♕xh5+ ♔d7 (for his sacrificed exchange Black has a slight bind and a potential kingside attack) 17 ♕h7+ ♗e7 18 ♖e1 ♖f8 19 ♖e4! ♘e5 20 ♔g2 ♘f7 21 ♗d2 ♖h8 22 ♕g7 ♕xf5 23 ♖xe7+! (not 23 ♕xf7?? ♕h3+ 24 ♔g1 ♕xh2+ 25 ♔f1 ♕h1+ 26 ♔e2 f3 mate) 23 ... ♔xe7 24 ♖e1+ (now the white king has an escape route) 24 ... ♔d8 25 ♕xf7 ♕h3+ 26 ♔g1 ♕xh2+ 27 ♔f1 ♕h3+ 28 ♔e2 ♖e8+ 29 ♔d1 ♕f3+ 30 ♔c1 ♖xe1+ 31 ♗xe1 ♕c6 32 b4! (White must open up the position for his bishop) 32 ... b6 33 ♕xa7 ♕e6 34 ♗d2 c4 35 dxc4 ♕xc4 36 ♕xb6+ and White won.

6	e4	d4

7	♘bd2	♘ge7
8	c4	

White wants to close the centre before advancing on the kingside. Bad for Black would be 8 ... dxc3 9 bxc3 with an active position for White. In the game Anic - Guigonis, French League 1991, White adopted another plan: 8 ♘c4 ♗c7 9 a4 h6 10 c3 g5 11 cxd4 cxd4 12 ♘e1 ♗e6 13 b3 ♕d7 14 ♗a3 0-0 15 b4 with advantage.

8	...	f6
9	♘h4	♗e6
10	f4	exf4
11	gxf4	♕c7
12	e5!	(128)

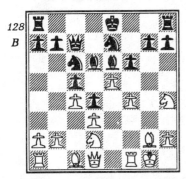

128
B

White sacrifices a pawn for a powerful outpost on e4 and a positional bind. As for Black, his 'extra' pawn on e5 merely deprives him of a useful square for his pieces.

12	...	fxe5
13	f5	♗f7
14	♘e4	0-0-0
15	♕g4!	

Threatening an unpleasant discovered check with 16 f6+.

15	...	♔b8

16	♕xg7	

It is not at all dangerous for White to open the g-file in front of his king, since Black's pieces are too badly placed to undertake active operations. Indeed, it is White who will attack on the kingside.

16	...	♗h5
17	♖f2	

Preventing 17 ... ♗e2.

17	...	h6
18	♗d2	♖dg8
19	♕f6	♘c8
20	♘g6!	

Cleverly forcing a blocking of the g-file.

20	...	♗xg6
21	fxg6	♗e7
22	♕f7	♘d8
23	♕f5	♗h4
24	♖f3	♘e7
25	♕h3	♘xg6 (129)

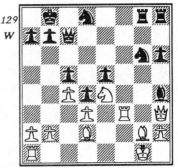

129
W

Having fulfilled its job as overseer, White's knight now clears the path for the king's bishop, eliminates Black's bishop and facilitates the invasion of the rooks into Black's position - all in one stroke.

26	♘f6!	♗xf6

27	♖xf6	♛e7
28	♖af1	♞f4
29	♖6xf4!	exf4

30	♗xf4+	1-0

30 ... ♚a8 31 ♛c8 mate.

8 Other Black Defences

Here too, the reader must be on the lookout for similarities with - and transpositional possibilities to - other lines. When White opens the game with ♘f3, g3 and ♗g2 Black can give the game a Queen's Indian flavour with ... b6 and ... ♗b7. Combine this with an early ... e6 and ... d5 and we could eventually arrive at a French Defence position. The same can be said of 1 ♘f3 ♘f6 2 g3 b5!? (see the ... 1 game). The other games in this chapter deal with hybrid positions which are only rarely encountered.

Benko - Bisguier
Stockholm Interzonal 1962

1	♘f3	♘f6
2	g3	d5
3	♗g2	e6
4	0-0	♗e7
5	d3	0-0
6	♘bd2	b6
7	e4 (130)	
7	...	♗b7

Making the central exchange with ... dxe4 can also be played in Queen's Indian positions. It has the advantage of increasing

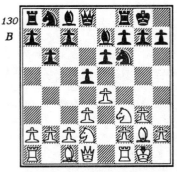

the scope of Black's queen's bishop and - in the event of e4 - e5 from White - securing a useful outpost on d5 for the king's knight. However, White's space advantage usually allows him freer movement of his pieces and thus eases the task of attacking the black king.

7 ... dxe4 8 dxe4 ♗b7 transposes to Rogers - Dutreeuw, Novi Sad Olympiad 1990. The game continued 9 e5 ♘d5 10 a3 (Black would stand better after 10 c4? ♘b4, but now White is indeed threatening to 'hit' the knight - hence Black's next) 10 ... b5 11 ♕e2 ♕d7 12 ♘e4 ♖e8 13 ♗g5 ♗f8 (instead of surrendering his dark-squared bishop Black prefers to use it as a defender) 14 ♘d4 a6 15 ♕g4 c5

16 ♘f3 ♕c7 17 ♖ad1 ♘d7 18 ♖fe1 (completing his development and indirectly defending the e-pawn, as 18 ... ♘xe5? 19 ♘xe5 ♕xe5 20 ♘xc5 ♕c7 21 ♘xb7 ♕xb7 gives Black problems down the h1 – a8 diagonal) 18 ... c4 19 ♖d4? (this allows Black to play 19 ... ♘xe5 20 ♘xe5 ♕xe5, e.g. 21 ♘f6+ ♘xf6; or 21 ♖xd5 exd5! 22 ♘f6+ ♕xf6! 23 ♗xf6 ♖xe1+) 19 ... c3? 20 b3 a5 (now White gets a second chance) 21 ♘f6+ ♘7xf6 22 exf6 ♖ad8 23 fxg7 ♗e7 (Black hopes to use the enemy pawn as a shield for his king, but White's queen's rook is too strong) 24 ♕h3 ♘f6 25 ♖f4 e5 26 ♗xf6 ♗c8 27 ♕h5 exf4 28 ♘g5 1-0.

| 8 | e5 | ♘fd7 |
| 9 | ♖e1 | ♖e8 |

Black should play 9 ... c5 followed by ... ♘c6 rather than concentrate on defensive measures at such an early stage of the game.

10	♘f1	♘f8
11	h4	♘bd7
12	♘1h2	c5
13	h5	h6 *(131)*

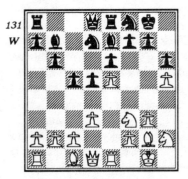

131
W

The position after 13 ... h6 greatly resembles King's Indian Attack vs French Defence games. An important difference is Black's lack of pressure on the queenside, whereas White has his usual prospects of a kingside attack.

| 14 | ♘g4 | ♘h7 |
| 15 | ♘fh2! | |

Aiming to keep Black's pieces from the g5-square with f2 – f4.

| 15 | ... | ♘df8 |
| 16 | f4 | ♖b8 |

At last Black begins to play on the queenside, but there are not enough pieces with which to cause White problems.

| 17 | ♗d2 | b5 |
| 18 | ♘f2 | d4? |

Very often in such positions it can be suicidal for Black to give his opponent full control of the e4-square. This game is no exception. More consistent is 18 ... a5 with a view to rolling the queenside pawns down the board, although White would still retain quite an advantage.

19	♗xb7	♖xb7
20	♕f3	♖d7
21	a4!	*(132)*

White strikes while Black's queenside is bereft of support. Black now has to choose between 21 ... a6 22 axb5 axb5, when the opening of the queenside favours White, or the game move.

| 21 | ... | b4 |
| 22 | b3 | |

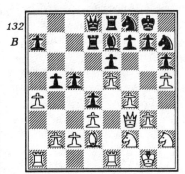

After this move it is the kingside which will become the main battlefield, so both sides set about regrouping their forces to maximum effect. White prepares to pounce, Black must do his best to be ready.

22	...	♖d5
23	♖e2	♘d7
24	♖ae1	♘b6
25	♘e4	♖d7
26	♕g4	♘d5
27	♖f1	♗f8
28	♘f3	♕b6 (133)

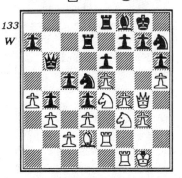

As a result of the 'shadow-boxing' Black's knight has journeyed from f8 to d5 and has subsequently been replaced by the bishop – in turn clearing

the second rank for the rook. White – who has had a strategically won game since move 19 – made richer gains, and his next move threatens a winning breakthrough with f4 – f5.

29	♘h4!	f5

Creating weaknesses, but Black had little choice.

30	exf6	♘hxf6
31	♘xf6+	♘xf6
32	♕g6	♕b8
33	♖fe1	♖de7
34	f5!	exf5

Not 34 ... e5 35 ♗xh6.

35	♖xe7	♖xe7
36	♖xe7	♗xe7
37	♘xf5	

White has kept his winning advantage even after the exchanges. The game concluded:

37	...	♗f8
38	♘xh6+	♔h8
39	♘f7+	♔g8
40	♗f4!	♕b7
41	♘h6+	♔h8
42	♘f7+	♔g8
43	♘g5!	♕e7
44	♗e5!	

Clever moves such as this make winning that much easier. Now 44 ... ♕xe5 loses the queen to 45 ♕f7+ ♔h8 46 ♕xf8+ ♘g8 47 ♘f7+. Instead, Black waits for his opponent to 'show' him the win.

44	...	♕e8
45	♗xf6	♕e1+

Or 45 ... ♕xg6 46 hxg6 gxf6 47 ♘e6, when Black's king is embarrassingly trapped, leaving

White free to win at will.

46	♔g2	♕e2+
47	♔h3	♕f1+
48	♔h4	♕h1+
49	♘h3	1-0

As one way of playing the King's Indian Attack involves developing the kingside pieces before disclosing one's intentions and embarking on a specific structural strategy, Black, too, is free to open in a number of ways. Spoilt for choice, Black occasionally goes too solid.

Damljanovic - Cvetkovic
Yugoslav Ch 1991

1	g3	d5
2	♗g2	♘f6
3	d3	g6
4	♘f3	♗g7
5	0-0	0-0
6	c3	c6 *(134)*

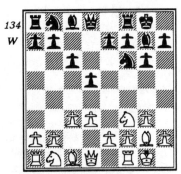

Perhaps this set-up is somewhat too conservative as White can freely expand on the queenside. More active is 6 ... c5 which transposes to the King's Indian Defence with colours

reversed. Another possibility is 6 ... ♘c6 followed by ... e5.

7	♘bd2	♘bd7
8	b4!	

Gaining space on the queenside and depriving Black of the c5-square.

8	...	e5
9	e4	dxe4
10	dxe4	a5
11	♕c2	♕c7
12	a4	♖e8
13	♖e1	♘b6
14	♘b3!	

In symmetrical positions White can often utilise the extra tempo to take the initiative. In this case White's pawn on b4 (as opposed to its counterpart on b7) is significant enough to give him the better game.

14	...	axb4
15	a5!	♘c4
16	cxb4	♘d6
17	♗b2	♘b5
18	h3!	*(135)*

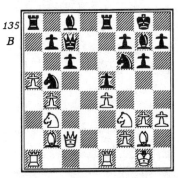

With Black's queen's knight attacking the d4-square White does not want to allow ... ♗g4 followed by ... ♗xf3.

18	...	♘d7
19	♗f1	

Threatening to win a piece with 20 ♗xb5.

19	...	♕d6
20	♕c4	♘f8
21	♖ad1	♗e6
22	♕c5!	♕b8!

Exchanging queens does not alleviate Black's problems.

23	♕c2	♗xb3

Black eliminates a potentially troublesome piece and makes way for his other knight to come to e6 and observe d4.

24	♕xb3	♘e6
25	♗xb5!	

Black was threatening to jump into 'd4'. Now, in return for his king's bishop, White will have the d5-square for his rook, attacking Black's weak pawns.

25	...	cxb5
26	♖d5	♕c7
27	♖c1	♕e7
28	♗xe5	

White chooses to take the e-pawn as the b-pawn will be the more difficult to defend.

28	...	♗xe5
29	♖xe5	♕f6
30	♔g2	♖ac8
31	♖xc8	♖xc8
32	♕d3!	

Not good is 32 ♖xb5 ♖c3! 33 ♕d1 ♖xf3 34 ♕xf3 ♕xf3+ 35 ♔xf3 ♘d4+ and 36 ... ♘xb5.

32	...	♖c4
33	♖xb5!?	♖c3
34	e5!	*(136)*

34 ♕d1 transposes to the

previous note. The game move vacates e4, thus assisting White's king on its journey to the queenside.

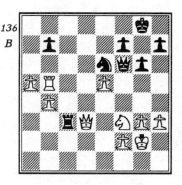

34	...	♕xf3+
35	♕xf3	♖xf3
36	♔xf3	♘d4+
37	♔e4	♘xb5
38	♔d5	♔f8
39	♔c5	♘c7
40	♔d6	♘b5+
41	♔c5	♘c7
42	♔d6	

Black can draw after 42 ♔b6? ♘d5+ 43 ♔xb7 ♘xb4 44 a6 ♘xa6 45 ♔xa6 ♔e7 because White's king is too far away from his pawns.

42	...	♘b5+
43	♔d7!	

White finds the correct continuation, heading for the b-pawn while simultaneously cutting off Black's king.

43	...	♘d4
44	♔c7	♘c2
45	b5	♘a3
46	b6	♔e7
47	a6	1-0

Petrosian – Donner
Santa Monica 1966

1	♘f3	d5
2	g3	g6
3	♗g2	♗g7
4	0–0	e5
5	d3	♘e7

Pachman's variation.

6	♘bd2	0–0
7	e4	c5?!

White can profit from this ambitious claim to the centre, so better is 7 ... dxe4, or maintaining the tension with 7 ... ♘bc6 (7 ... c6 transposes to the Caro-Kann Defence). Instead Botvinnik – Pachman, Leipzig Olympiad 1960, went 7 ... d4 8 a4 f6 9 ♘h4 ♗e6 10 f4 ♘d7 11 f5 ♗f7 12 fxg6 hxg6 13 ♗h3 with a clear advantage to White.

8	exd5	♘xd5
9	♘b3!	

Rather than play the normal 9 ♘c4 ♘c6 White punishes his opponent's move order by attacking the c-pawn.

9	...	♘d7

9 ... b6 is not possible as it opens the long h1 – a8 diagonal, which Black sets about clearing.

10	♖e1	♖b8
11	♘fd2!	♘c7
12	♘a5!	♘e6

Black's intended 12 ... b6 loses to 13 ♘c6.

13	♘ac4	♕c7

White is better after 13 ... b6 14 ♘d6 ♗a6 15 a4, meeting 15 ... ♕c7 with 16 ♘b5.

14 ♘e4! *(137)*

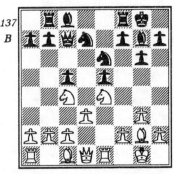

137
B

14	...	♘b6

Again 14 ... b6 15 ♘ed6 ♗a6 16 a4 is good for White (as in the last note). Black does have an active plan in 14 ... b5 15 ♘cd6 ♗a6 16 a4 f5, but 17 axb5 fxe4 18 ♖xa6! is crushing. This leads us to 16 ... b4 with a slight edge for White thanks to the c4-square.

15	♘c3	

Threatening a future ♘b5 and watching over d5.

15	...	♗d7
16	a4	♗c6

Tempting White into what he anyway intended, and thus effectively losing a tempo. 16 ... ♘d4 or 16 ... ♖fd8 are less compromising.

17	♘b5	♗xb5
18	axb5	♘xc4
19	dxc4	b6 *(138)*

On studying the diagram position we see that White has reaped several benefits from his imaginative knight manoeuvres. Black's a-pawn is a chronic weakness against which Petrosian can build up pressure at will. White's king's bishop is excellently placed, and the absence of its black counterpart accentuates the domination of the white squares – notably the long diagonal.

20	c3	♖fe8
21	♖a6	♖e7

Black gets ready to defend his a-pawn.

22	♕a4	♖c8
23	♗d5!	♕b8

Or 23 ... ♘d8 24 ♗g5 ♖d7 25 ♗c6 when Black's position is over-loaded.

24 ♗xe6!

Now Black will either lose his a-pawn or have to spoil his pawn structure. Against a positional player of Petrosian's calibre perhaps the former is the lesser evil, but Donner is in material mood.

24	...	fxe6
25	♕d1!	♖d8
26	♕g4	

White has more than one target to aim at.

26	...	♖ee8
27	h4!	♖d7
28	h5	gxh5

29	♕xh5	♖f8
30	♕g4	♖f6

Petrosian suggested 30 ... ♖f5 followed by ... h5.

31	♗e3	♖g6
32	♕e4	♘f8
33	♖aa1	

The queen's rook has no further role to play on the a-file.

33	...	♗d6
34	♖ed1	♖gg7
35	♖d2	♗f8
36	♖xd7	♖xd7
37	♕g4+	♔f7
38	♕h3	♔f6

Otherwise Black loses a pawn. Now 39 ♕h5 is the most accurate continuation, threatening 40 ♗g5+ and 41 ♗h6+.

39	♖f1	♕e8
40	♕h4+	♔g7
41	♗h6+	♔g8
42	♗xf8	

Without his bishop Black will have problems defending the e5-pawn. Recapturing with the queen does not help: 42 ... ♕xf8 43 ♕g4+ ♔f7 44 ♕h5+ ♔f6 45 ♖e1.

42	...	♔xf8
43	♖e1	♕f7
44	♖xe5	♕g6
45	♔g2!	♕f7
46	♖e4!	

Apart from being a pawn down, Black has other weak pawns and no shelter for his king. The game finished:

46	...	♔e8
47	♖f4	♕e7
48	♕h5+	♔d8

49 ♕e5   ♔c8

White threatened 50 ♕b8 mate.

50 ♕e4

Threatening 51 ♕a8+ ♔c7 52 ♕xa7+.

50 ...   ♔b8
51 ♖h4   ♕f7

To defend the e-pawn with ... ♖e7.

52 ♖f4   ♕e7
53 ♕f3   ♕d6
54 ♖f8+   ♖d8

If 54 ... ♔c7 55 ♕a8 wins.

55 ♖f6

Black resigned as 55 ... ♖d7 56 ♕e4 ♖e7 (The e-pawn must be defended) 57 ♖f8+ ♔c7 58 ♕a8 leads to mate.

Bilek – Tal
Moscow 1967

1 ♘f3   ♘f6
2 g3   b5!? *(139)*

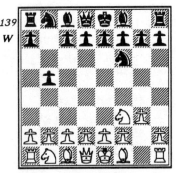

If this seems bizarre it is worth mentioning that Spassky was adventurous enough to play it against Petrosian in their 1966 World Championship match! Petrosian immediately

struck on the queenside with 3 a4, but after 3 ... b4 4 d3 ♗b7 5 e4 d6 6 ♗g2 ♘bd7 7 0-0 e6 8 a5 ♖b8 9 ♘bd2 ♗e7 10 ♘c4 0-0 11 ♖e1 a6 12 ♗f4 ♗a8 13 ♕e2?! ♖e8! Black had the upper hand. Although 13 e5 improves, it seems better to keep a2 – a4 in reserve.

3 ♗g2   ♗b7
4 0-0   e6
5 d3

A direct course is 5 c3 c5 6 ♕b3!?, when 6 ... ♕b6 keeps White's edge to a minimum, while 6 ... ♗c6 is doubtful because of 7 d3 d6 8 ♗g5 ♗e7 9 ♘fd2! ♗xg2 10 ♔xg2 a6 11 ♗xf6! ♗xf6 12 a4 with advantage to White, Gutman – Grünfeld, Israel 1985.

5 ...   d5
6 ♘bd2   ♗e7
7 e4   0-0

7 ... dxe4 8 ♘g5 favours White.

8 ♕e2   c5
9 ♖e1   ♘c6
10 c3

The reader may notice – and by now will not be surprised – that it is possible for White to transpose to a French Defence line here with 10 e5. However, Bilek prefers to punish Black's provocative move order, planning to use the f5-square and the e-file.

10 ...   a5
11 exd5   exd5
12 d4   ♕b6
13 dxc5   ♗xc5

14 ♘b3   ♖fe8
15 ♕c2   d4

Opening the long diagonal for his favourite bishop, and avoiding 15 ... ♗f8 16 ♗e3.

16 ♕f5!   ♖xe1+
17 ♘xe1   ♖e8
18 ♘f3?

White follows Black's lead and enters into complications; effectively playing into Tal's hands. However, 18 ♗f4 ensures the safe capture of the black d-pawn.

18 ...   ♗d6
19 ♗g5   ♘e4
20 ♖e1   ♘e7 *(140)*

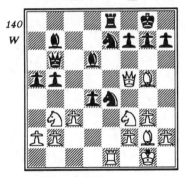

21 ♗xe7

Equally manic is 21 ♖xe4 ♘xf5 22 ♖xe8+ ♗f8 23 ♘e5, hoping for the remarkable variation 23 ... ♕c7 24 ♗xb7 ♕xb7 25 ♘c5 ♕d5 26 ♘cd7 h6 27 ♘xf8 hxg5 28 ♘g6+ ♔h7 29

♖h8+. Unfortunately for White, 24 ... ♘d6 holds Black's position together.

21 ...   g6!
22 ♕h3   dxc3!

The winning move. After mass exchanges this pawn would decide: 23 ♗xd6 ♕xf2+ 24 ♔h1 ♕xe1+ 25 ♘xe1 ♘f2+ 26 ♔g1 ♘xh3+ 27 ♔f1 ♗xg2+ 28 ♘xg2 cxb2! 29 ♘d2 ♖d8!.

23 ♖xe4   cxb2!

Not 23 ... ♗xe4 24 ♘g5.

24 ♖e1   ♖xe7
25 ♖b1   a4
26 ♘bd4   ♗xf3
27 ♘xf3   ♖e2
28 ♖f1   ♖xf2!
29 ♕c8+   ♔g7
30 ♕c3+   f6
0-1

An important lesson with which to end! White was thrown off balance by his opponent's second move and subsequently let himself get drawn into a web of tactics. Preferable is 5 c3, mentioned above, or at any rate a more level-headed approach than Bilek's. Transposition into the French Defence variation is also a good idea, and in my opinion the best, since we are then back onto familiar ground.

Index of Complete Games